HE COULD NOT DO OTHERWISE

He Could Not Do Otherwise

Bishop Lajos Ordass, 1901-1978

László G. Terray

Translated from the German by
Eric W. Gritsch

WILLIAM B. EERDMANS PUBLISHING COMPANY
GRAND RAPIDS, MICHIGAN / CAMBRIDGE, U.K.

This translation of the original German edition
(*In königlicher Freiheit. Bischof Lajos Ordass, 1901-1978*
[Erlangen: Martin Luther Verlag, 1990])
© 1997 Wm. B. Eerdmans Publishing Co.
255 Jefferson Ave. S.E., Grand Rapids, Michigan 49503 /
P.O. Box 163, Cambridge CB3 9PU U.K.
All rights reserved

Printed in the United States of America

02 01 00 99 98 97   7 6 5 4 3 2 1

Library of Congress Cataloging-in-Publication Data

Terray, László G.
   [In königlicher Freiheit. English]
   He could not do otherwise : Bishop Lajos Ordass, 1901-1978 /
László G. Terray : translated from the German by Eric W. Gritsch.
     p.   cm.
   Includes bibliographical references and index.
   ISBN 0-8028-4318-2 (pbk. : alk. paper)
   1. Ordass, Lajos, 1901-1978. 2. Lutheran Church — Hungary —
Bishops — Biography. 3. Magyarországi Evangélikus Egyház —
Bishops — Biography. I. Title.
BX8080.0715T47 1997
284.1'092 — dc21   97-12966
[B]   CIP

Contents

Translator's Preface	vii
Preface to the German Edition	viii
1. The Police Are Knocking	1
2. Son of "the Strict Teacher"	3
3. Death of a Village	7
4. Education	10
5. Teacher or Pastor?	14
6. Student and Miner	17
7. A Year in Sweden	23
8. A Congregation Flourishes	28
9. War Years in Budapest	35
10. Bishop in Hard Times	42
11. Travels	49
12. Ecumenical Responsibility	55
13. Dark Clouds on the Horizon	60
14. As If a Curtain Had Opened	66
15. A Matter of Identity and Integrity	72

16. A Mock Trial	80
17. The Cell of the Priests	86
18. The "New Era" in the Church	91
19. In Solitary Confinement	97
20. A Disciplinary Matter	102
21. Only a Spectator	107
22. Thaw in Hungary	115
23. Once Again, a New Beginning	120
24. Minneapolis, 1957	126
25. "Is the Informer More Reliable than the Bishop?"	130
26. Deposed a Second Time	135
27. An East European State Church	142
28. A Diary Loses Its Way	147
29. "Worthy of Your Calling"	151
30. Witness of Christ for Our Time	155
Epilogue	157
Sources and Literature	160
Chronology	163
Index	166

Translator's Preface

THE STORY of Hungarian resistance to Adolf Hitler's Nazism and Joseph Stalin's Communism is not well known. It cannot be told without reference to the Hungarian Lutheran bishop Lajos Ordass. I translated this book from German in order to make part of the story known to English-speaking readers. The title is taken from the Norwegian edition.

Bishop Ordass was quite well known after World War II, when he was involved in the ecumenical movement. Influenced by one of its greatest pioneers, Archbishop Nathan Söderblom of Uppsala (1866-1931), Bishop Ordass established a strong link between Hungary and global Christianity. He was a member of the Central Committee of the World Council of Churches from its inception in 1948 until 1954. He also served as vice president of the Lutheran World Federation in 1947 and 1957. Muhlenberg College awarded him an honorary doctorate in 1947.

As a son of a Hungarian Lutheran pastor in Austria, I continue to honor my past through this translation, a labor of love. I have learned much about the significance of Bishop Ordass through my work on the Board of Directors of the Ordass Foundation in Oslo, Norway. The German Lutheran martyr Dietrich Bonhoeffer alerted the world to learn about "the underside of history," the story of the persecuted. Bishop Ordass was one of these. Like his spiritual ancestor Martin Luther at Worms in 1521, Ordass made a stand for the freedom of the gospel against seemingly impossible odds. He, too, could not do otherwise.

On the eve of All Saints' Day, October 31, 1996
EWG

Preface to the German Edition

SINCE THE publication of this biography in the spring of 1984 by the Luther Publishing House in Oslo, much has changed in Europe and especially in the so-called peoples' democratic countries in Eastern Europe. Nevertheless, not only will a presentation of the life and work of Lajos Ordass not be out of date; it may, on the contrary, be more relevant than before.

New sources for the history of Lajos Ordass and the Lutheran church in Hungary have been made available during the last four decades. It will be the task of church historians to supplement, indeed to correct, the picture portrayed in this book. The most important basis for this book was the autobiographical notes of Lajos Ordass, *Small Mirror for Great Times (Nagy idők kis tükre)*. They were available at the time of the origin of this book (1983) only in a manuscript owned by the Ordass Foundation in Norway. In the meantime, these notes have been published, though in Hungarian, in two volumes with extensive explanatory notes by Pastor István Szépfalusi (*Önéletrajzi Írások* [Bern, 1985 and 1987]). It is my hope that the present book will fill a gap in the presentations of recent East European church history.

A special word of thanks is due to Ingalisa Reicke, Basel, for the translation of the Norwegian original edition into German. The newly elected president of the Union of Lutheran Churches (Bund der evangelisch-lutherischen Kirchen) in Switzerland and in the principality of Liechtenstein has rendered a great service to the communion of Lutheran churches and the general public interested in the church.

PREFACE TO THE GERMAN EDITION

Moreover, thanks are due to friends and co-workers all over Europe for having provided photographic material for this book.

Not least, thanks are due to my wife, Unni, who has accompanied the whole labor with the greatest patience and goodwill.

Råde, Norway, June 1990
L. G. Terray

1. The Police Are Knocking

THE TWO policemen on duty made their usual rounds in the village. It was 2:00 a.m. Everything seemed quiet and peaceful.

Torzsa was generally a peaceful place. Its three thousand inhabitants projected an image of stability, continuity, and tradition. Most of them were peasants who owned their land, or craftsmen of German immigrant stock. German settlers had come to southern Hungary at the end of the eighteenth century. Under Turkish domination for centuries, this part of Hungary had been only thinly settled until Emperor Franz Joseph II had offered land grants to Germans who wanted to settle there. That is how Torzsa was founded, along with a series of other small towns and villages in the Batschka region.

The influx of foreigners steadily increased during the subsequent century. Hungarian authorities constructed a large canal, linking the two main rivers, the Danube and the Theiss, thus cutting the distance to the Black Sea and enabling more traffic on smaller waterways. An extension of the canal, named after Emperor Franz Joseph, was constructed not far from Torzsa. At the same location a railway line crossed the canal. So there was a bit more traffic than before.

But this situation did not create more work for the voluntary police force recruited by the local population. Torzsa was a peaceful place. Making their rounds, the policemen saw light shining through the windows of the home of teacher Wolf. What was going on there? Had unwelcome guests come, trying to take the teacher's food and clothes? The policemen hesitated a few moments and contemplated what to do. Finally, one of them knocked at the window. The teacher quickly appeared and explained the situation. No, there were no unwelcome guests. Quite the contrary. The midwife had arrived to help Mrs. Wolf in the birthing of a son. The third son among five in the family.

During the nearly two years that the future bishop Lajos Ordass had to spend in prison because of his Christian convictions, he frequently thought of the visit of the two policemen during the night of his birth. A strange coincidence that the police were knocking already on February 6, 1901.

2. Son of "the Strict Teacher"

Lajos Ordass or Wolf, his original name, had a happy childhood. His father, Arthur Wolf, was a native of Korompa in northern Hungary (now part of Slovakia) and had come to the Batschka region in 1895, right after he had completed his education as a teacher. After conscientious work in several other congregations, he was called in 1898 as teacher and organist to the Lutheran congregation in Torzsa. He stayed there until his death in 1935.

Arthur Wolf had married Paula Steinmetz in his earlier place of employment, Zsablya. She was the daughter of an older colleague of Wolf's. Four children were born there: Arthur, Paula, János, and Ilona. Lajos was the fifth child, followed by a sister, Matild. The Lutheran teacher lived in the schoolhouse of Torzsa, with a piece of land in the back that he could use it in whatever way he wished as part of his salary. The Reformed teacher had the same contract. Both denominations had about the same number of members, and each had its own church, located across from each other on the main street in the center of town.

Wolf's salary was not large, so he and his wife supplemented their income with other work. Wolf increased the yield of his land by raising bees and silkworms. He also went hunting in the fall. Mrs. Wolf offered craft courses every summer for thirty or forty girls. Their parents paid her with sugar from their own fields of sugar beets. Even though there were many mouths to feed, no one suffered in the teacher's home. But little could be afforded beyond daily needs.

Lajos spent the first ten years of his life in Torzsa. Both of his parents had many interests. Order and discipline marked the home.

Arthur Wolf was known as "the strict teacher." But order and discipline were shaped by hearty love and strong togetherness. All of the children were put to work. The first thing young Lajos had to learn was weeding, removing weeds from the path in the big garden. He also had to help out in the vegetable garden and in the orchard, as well as with the bees and in the vineyard that was part of the property. For a whole year he and his younger sister tried to produce their own silk. It was hard work to feed the silkworms, but they were successful. They were able to buy a pair of shoes with the money they made, a very welcome strengthening of the family's finances. Young Lajos also learned how to sew in his mother's craft course for girls. All these skills came in handy later when he was imprisoned, and also in the years when he was deprived of salary, pension, and other income and had to provide for his family with practical work.

There were many bright moments in the life at home, which was generally marked by moderation and hard work. During the summer Lajos could spend afternoons swimming in the canal with friends, but first he had to take the annual school examinations. These exams were a solemn occasion. They took place in the church, before the assembled congregation. It was no small effort to answer questions with the attention of the whole congregation upon him. But afterward the joy was even greater, for the whole world seemed to have opened up.

He was allowed to swim every day except Sunday. Lajos learned how to swim at such an early age that he could not remember his first swimming strokes. When the adults also came to swim toward evening, the boy often ferried them across to the other side of the canal where the bath house was located. Occasionally there was money in it, a welcome addition to the meager family income.

In the fall, a fair was held in connection with the commemoration of the dedication of the church. The occasion attracted many outsiders to Torzsa. The stalls were erected in front of the school. Relatives from distant places came to visit. There was dancing for three days in the local inns. Fewer people showed up at Sunday worship services, but the village was filled with life.

Young Lajos had fun working as a "pusher" at one of the merry-go-rounds. The merry-go-rounds were kept moving by muscle power. The "pusher" got a free ride after five rounds. This helped both sides: the owner did not have to pay a wage, and the boys did not have to use their money for the rides. But the highlight of the fair was the job of cleaning up when the fair had ended. The boys searched the dusty sand, or mud in the case of rain, for coins lost during the fair. Sometimes they collected a neat little sum that rightfully belonged to the finders.

During the long winter evenings, teacher families from the region gathered together. The women worked at crafts, the men talked politics, and the children played in a corner. Sometimes there was the "plucking of the geese," that is, the sorting out of feathers for bed covers and pillows. When the oldest Wolf daughter got married, her dowry was readied during such evenings. During the work a book or magazine was read aloud, and when the work was finished there were party games interspersed with humorous stories.

In the winter there was the enticing ice on the canal. But the price of a pair of skates was beyond the limits of the small budget of a teacher. By chance young Lajos found a single skate, but its screws were stuck in the rust. He was able to fasten the skate to one shoe with the help of a thin rope. That at least gave him the feeling of skating by using the skate on one foot and a skateless shoe on the other. But he never mastered skating that way. He saw his first bicycle during the summer vacation after the first grade in elementary school. A prosperous farmer had bought this strange means of transportation for his son, who was probably the only boy in Torzsa who mastered the art of bicycling. The other boys had fun running behind him, breathing in the dust that even such a simple means of transportation could stir up.

The Wolf family rarely traveled to new areas. Once a year Lajos's father traveled a few miles to the nearest town in order to sell his silkworms. Occasionally, Lajos could accompany him. His first trip by train took him to the town of Palánka, about twenty miles south of Torzsa. An uncle of Lajos's mother practiced law there. There Lajos saw the Danube for the first time, and he was even allowed to swim in the large river.

Even though travel was limited, there were visitors from afar. Arthur Wolf's father traveled all the way from northern Hungary, and an aunt came from Debrecen. Moreover, Arthur Wolf encouraged a student exchange: his daughters would go to a Hungarian school for citizens in Orosháza; students from there would come to Torzsa in the summer to learn German.

The thrift and hard work of the Wolf family was rooted in their solid Christian Lutheran faith. Arthur Wolf was not just employed by the church; he also lived in the church. Lajos's parents viewed hard work as worship, and they taught their children the solid belief that God dwelled in their home. Already as a small boy Lajos was permitted to accompany his father to church when he did his work as an organist. Lajos was able to help now and then, but most of the time he was probably in the way. But he learned from early childhood on that it was not really Sunday if one had not attended church.

The church in Torzsa left lasting impressions that affected Lajos all his life. His pastor, Gustav Adolf Famler, was one of the many diligent and conscientious pastors in the Lutheran Church of Hungary. Ordass always spoke of him with great respect. The son of the pastor also became his friend. Pastor Famler initiated, among other things, the building of an orphanage in Torzsa; it became an important institution of the Lutheran Church.

The alterpiece in the church of Torzsa, which depicted the suffering Jesus on the cross, was probably the memory of his childhood that was most deeply impressed on his mind. The picture was imprinted in his mind when he was a child; it inspired him as an adult when he spoke and wrote; and it consoled him in the difficult years of trial.

3. Death of a Village

THE FIRST inhabitants of Torzsa, 249 families, settled there at the end of the eighteenth century on the basis of an edict of Emperor Franz Joseph II. They came mainly from the Palatinate and became commonly known as "Swabians." Torzsa was not the only place to originate that way.

The inhabitants were hardworking people. Above all, they were outstanding farmers who grew wheat, corn, flax, and sugar beets. Torzsa was the first region in Hungary to begin experimenting with rice growing. Many farmers later grew their own rice. Farmers from Torzsa earned prizes at the agricultural fairs in the province and in the country. One farmer even began exporting pigs to other countries.

The population of Torzsa was, on the whole, of German descent. Only the stationmaster and the swineherd were of Hungarian descent during Lajos's childhood and youth. But in each new generation the influence of Hungarian culture and language increased. That was mainly due to the government's ruthless policy of "Hungarianization." The Hungarian language had to be used in the schools. The school of Torzsa taught German as an extra. Thus Hungarian increasingly became the language of daily life. The majority of the adults in Torzsa were bilingual. Many of them increasingly believed that they would have to give up part of their original identity since they had now found their home in this part of Europe.

Those who had attended schools beyond elementary school belonged to an association that furthered Hungarian culture and language. They organized the production of plays and discussions in the evenings, and they maintained their own Hungarian library. When the village was annexed to Yugoslavia at the end of World War I, most of the inhabitants called themselves Hungarian, even though some had to make that statement in German!

Arthur Wolf belonged to those who consciously labored to strengthen the bonds to the Hungarian homeland. He wanted Hungary to be viewed as the true fatherland. When his son Lajos was asked to transfer to the German-speaking Bruckenthal Gymnasium in Hermannstadt (now Sibiu, Romania), the intellectual center of the Romanian (Siebenburger) Saxons — after graduating with distinction from the intermediate grade — his father would not hear of it. "I do not wish you to become a 'Pan-German,'" he said. This made a lasting impression on Lajos and strengthened his affectionate ties to the Hungarian Lutheran Church.

The fact that Lajos was bilingual was very helpful in his future service, for it enabled him to learn other Western European languages, such as English and Scandinavian languages, with ease. The "Hungarianization" of Torzsa was not very successful. When the propaganda for a new Germany (Reich) reached the villages of the Batschka region, many inhabitants had a change of heart directed against Hungary and Yugoslavia. When Lajos occasionally came home to Torzsa during the 1930s he found that the village was increasingly visited by Germans. The visitors consisted of journalists, professors, businessmen, farmers, and technicians. Near the end of the decade whole groups of young men and women hiked through the "Swabian" villages to carry on propaganda for their nationalist ideals, not without success.

Lajos detected the actual character of the ideology behind the propaganda. But there certainly were some people in his old hometown who thought that in the newly ordered Europe this part of Yugoslavia would be included in the great new Germany. Soon it would become evident that the great German dream was a figment of the imagination.

The political stance of many Torzsa inhabitants resulted in much hatred and distrust. Most of them could not remain in their home country after the defeat of Germany. In the fall of 1944, a long trek of wagons from Torzsa and many other villages moved to Germany. Some old and naive folk stayed, thinking that they would not be punished for something they had not done. That was a deadly error. When the Serbs came to power, after four years of German occupation, they wanted revenge. And when they could not find the guilty ones, they revenged themselves on those who were still there. The inhabitants of Torzsa and the surrounding area were sent into prison camps, which often consisted of nothing but a field fenced in with barbed wire. After a few months their fate was sealed there.

One hundred and fifty years of Torzsa's history came to a tragic end. A new generation, raised as refugees in Germany or Austria, knew their homeland only through stories told by parents and grandparents. Two impressive volumes of local history still testify to the history of Torzsa, in which the Wolf family has earned a well-deserved place.

After the war, settlers from overpopulated regions in the south of Yugoslavia moved to the empty village; the name of the village was changed to Savino Selo. The old farms became collective enterprises.

The large Lutheran church, dating from 1810, was torn down after World War II. The small minority still loyal to the church could no longer bear the financial burden of the large building. Now and then, a Reformed pastor from the district capital, Verbász, conducts services in the Reformed church. Savino Selo is no longer Torzsa.

4. Education

IN THE Hungarian school system, already after the fourth or fifth grade a student had to choose one of three forms of education: eight years at the gymnasium or secondary school, with the goal of acceptance for university studies; four years of secondary elementary school, which qualified the student for further vocational education; or a so-called civic school, also for four years, as a basis for a career in business or in teaching. The financial situation of the parents frequently decided the choice of school or vocation for a child.

The village teacher certainly was not among the rich. But if he was able to use his piece of land well and could earn additional income, it was possible to get his children into the gymnasium or even to the university. And Arthur Wolf was one of those capable village teachers. One of his sons became a phycisian in Torzsa; another succeeded him as teacher and organist there. Both also served in various offices in the village and in the church.

It was not the custom at that time to provide a similar education for the daughters. One was satisfied if they married "well." But Arthur Wolf's two daughters were allowed to attend the "civic school." Later they also married well.

The youngest son, Lajos, ended up furthest away from his hometown, across the national border that had been established after World War I. He spent his first five years of school in Torzsa. His father was the teacher during the final year. In addition he had violin lessons. Playing the violin became a source of great joy for him during the many years when he was suspended from church service. The elementary school teacher was his first music teacher; he later married Lajos's sister Paula. At the time of the wedding Lajos was only ten years old. During the celebration Lajos was inadvertently given too much wine, so that he was downright drunk. As a result of this experience, Lajos was very careful with alcoholic beverages throughout his life, although he would not refuse a glass of wine in good company.

After five years in elementary school, Lajos attended the gymnasium in Verbász. The town was only thirteen miles from Torzsa, but still too far to commute every day by means of the transportation of the time. So he was housed, with five other students, with a friend from his father's youth. This friend was not married, and his younger sister took care of the house. The faculty of the Verbász Gymnasium did not come up to the most modern pedagogical standards, but young Ordass liked the school. He was allowed to play in the school orchestra in the cello section. His academic record was excellent at the end of the school year.

The gymnasium was financed partly by the government and partly by the town. All students, regardless of religious affiliation, had to attend courses in religion. Lutherans were in the great majority in the school in Verbász. Lutherans in Hungary had the least percentage of illiterate people and the greatest number of academically trained people. The local Lutheran vicar was the instructor of religion at the gymnasium. He especially stressed knowledge of Holy Scripture. Lajos took this to heart and read the whole Bible in the first year. At this time he also earned a regular income by tutoring other students.

World War I began during the summer vacation after Lajos's first grade in the gymnasium. Two of his brothers and his brother-in-law were drafted. Part of the school in Verbász was transformed into a field hospital. The wounded from the Balkan front were treated there. The war with all its consequences soon became repugnant to the young student. The war ended in the complete defeat of the Austro-Hungarian monarchy.

After three years, Arthur Wolf had his son transferred to the Lutheran gymnasium in Bonyhád, ninety-three miles north of Torzsa. Lajos discovered the reason for the change only after many years. His grades in religion, at Christmas and also at the end of the school year, had been bad. At the time his father shook his head and said, "Next year you are not going to Verbász." Many years later he told his son that he had had a quarrel with the religion teacher in the third grade at a church convention. Obviously, the teacher wanted to seek revenge by giving the son bad grades.

Bonyhád was too far away for his father or mother to accompany the boy at the beginning of the school year. He was then fourteen and had to enroll himself at the school as well as reporting to the principal. He also had to move himself into the dormitory. There he lived with about one hundred other students, receiving full board for a moderate sum that was determined by academic excellence.

The gymnasium in Bonyhád was one of the best schools maintained by the Lutheran Church. Moreover, it had the reputation of being among the best schools in the country. Universities as well as a large number of schools were owned by the various churches in Hungary at that time. The religious schools had a very good reputation. When Ordass later, as bishop, defended the independence of the religious schools, he knew quite well what was at stake — he himself had attended one of the best of these schools.

The war and the postwar situation shaped the curriculum during Lajos's five years at the gymnasium in Bonyhád. Many teachers had been drafted; vicars and students filled in as best they could. Classes were interrupted by "firewood vacations" or shortened by extensions of winter and Easter vacations. Drawing and gymnastics were dropped during those five years. Yet a good deal of learning still went on at Bonyhád, despite such shortages, which were typical of most of the Hungarian schools during the war years.

At the end of May 1916, shortly before the end of Lajos's first year in Bonyhád, Ordass was called to see the principal. The principal, visibly shaken, told him that Lajos's mother had died the day before. Lajos's return home to his family, as well as the funeral, left an indelible impression. Both of Lajos's brothers and his brother-in-law were in the war. The rest of the family seemed paralyzed. A sudden cloudburst at the graveside drenched everybody. The summer vacation was sad — and it was the last Lajos was to spend with his relatives.

Two years later the war ended. The Austro-Hungarian monarchy was gone, and significant parts of Hungary were annexed by the neighboring states — Czechoslovakia, Romania, and Yugoslavia. Several hundred thousand Hungarian citizens were now ruled by governments that had been enemies during the war. Oppression of ethnic minorities by those governments was worse than the oppression by the Hungarian government had been.

From this time on, Torzsa belonged to Yugoslavia, while Bonyhád remained in independent Hungary. As a consequence, Lajos was cut off from contact with his family in Torzsa for the next five years. The borders remained hermetically sealed for years. Neither letters nor packages nor money could be sent. Thus a totally new segment began in the life of the seventeen-year-old Lajos Ordass.

5. Teacher or Pastor?

FORTUNATELY, LAJOS was permitted to stay in the boarding school. He paid only a moderate sum for board because of his good academic record during his first three years. He tutored several students in order to cover his expenses and to have a bit of pocket money. But because he liked playing in the orchestra and also volunteered for several enterprises, his days were so filled that often he had time for homework only after the other students had gone to bed.

He was most concerned about his very poor wardrobe. He had to patch and mend the few clothes he had since he could not afford to buy something new. His mother's instructions in needlework enabled him to mend underwear, socks, and gloves. He had "inherited" two well-worn suits from his brothers, but he soon outgrew one suit, while the other was still too big. He also had a used "Sunday suit" from his brother-in-law, which fit so badly that everybody grinned when they saw him in it. But the suit would have to serve him for another seven years, until the end of his studies. He cared for it so loyally that he considered composing a hymn of praise for this well-used article of clothing.

Lajos had to decide the direction of his studies without being able to get advice from his family. Clearly, he wanted to continue his studies. He came through his last two years at the gymnasium with the help of other students and their families, even though his academic record was no longer excellent. The struggle for survival had cost much time and energy.

Since childhood he had been inclined toward the ordained ministry. Some of his friends in the gymnasium decided for it. But he doubted whether he was fit for this vocation, since he felt unable to appear before a large assembly. He was quite able to recite poetry by heart before his own class in school. But when his teacher appointed him to recite the same poems at a school festival, he failed. Twice he had to retreat blushingly from the platform without succeeding in his task. How could he ever step into a pulpit?

The mathematics teacher suggested that he should become a gymnasium teacher. When he received his matriculation certificate in the spring of 1919, he immediately applied for admission at the Mathematics and Science Faculty at the University of Budapest. But competition for placement proved to be too strong. A never-ending stream of refugees poured into Hungary from regions that Hungary had had to surrender to neighboring states, and the educational facilities had far more applicants than openings. To be on the safe side, Lajos also sent an application to the Lutheran Theological Academy in Budapest. He was accepted there.

During his early years, Lajos Ordass was not accustomed to speak much about God's leading, divine providence, or divine intervention. But later he began to understand his choice of vocation, like any other event, as being led by God.

There had not been a Lutheran theological educational facility in Budapest. Before World War I, the Lutheran Church in Hungary had three theological academies: one in Sopron (Ödenburg), another in Pressburg (Pozsony), now Bratislava, and the third in Eperjes (Presov). When new borders were established after the war, the cities in which the two last-mentioned academies were located became part of Czechoslovakia. So both institutions "fled." To be sure, they could not take with them buildings or libraries, or any other equipment. It was simply the faculty, or a portion of it, that fled to what was left of Hungary, in part followed by students. Curriculum and space were very limited. The University of Budapest offered six classrooms in one building for their use. Three of the rooms were used to house students; two professors and their families lived in two other rooms; and the remaining room was reserved for teaching. Twelve to fifteen students were to be housed in each room, but there was insufficient space, so some of the entering students had to sleep in the hallway. There were no reading rooms, writing desks, closets, indeed no chairs, and this had negative consequences for studies.

Lajos and two of his former fellow students also enrolled in a "refugee university." It functioned in parallel with the venerable three-hundred-year-old University of Budapest. But it had few students because it had some deficiences, as did the Theological Academy: no library, little equipment, and hardly any personnel. But its students had one great advantage: they were permitted to use the large reading room of the university library, which was heated, as Lajos gratefully discovered.

At this time, the path to the ordained ministry led Lajos to a conscious decision. At the "refugee university" he studied languages as the scientific basis for the study of theology, which would become his lifelong task.

Lajos secured the necessary finances for his studies through tutoring. Housing was free for theology students, as were the meals in the student's refectory, financed through sister churches abroad, but the food was not substantial or sufficient. One of the professors needs to be remembered in this connection, not so much because of his theological abilities, but because of his warm heart. The Old Testament professor, János Deák, helped the students obtain additional food by taking them to congregations to preach and sing. Most of the time they returned with heavy bags filled with potatoes, vegetables, flour, eggs, fruit, and even meat.

Lajos also had a few good memories about these "supply trips." The whole enterprise needed to be organized with the help of an episcopal circular letter in order to be successful. Professor Deák composed these letters to the congregations; they were then reproduced by the hands of students and signed by the bishop. When the bishop, Sándor Raffay, who was later internationally known, was presented with a letter to sign that had been reproduced by Ordass, he looked at the graceful handwriting and said angrily, "You have to get this guy out of the Academy. Whoever wastes so much time creating letters will never do good work." That was the first utterance of Bishop Raffay about the man who was to be his successor.

6. Student and Miner

During his second year of studies, Lajos applied for a scholarship to study in Germany. He hoped to find better working conditions there, to improve his German, and to get to know the world a bit better.

He was overjoyed when he was granted a stipend of 210 deutsche marks (about $160). In addition, he was promised a reduction of cost when staying at the famous Francke institutions in Halle. The prospect of studying there seemed to be favorable to Ordass. The granted stipend was to cover the cost for a stay of eight months. He had no idea that this stipend would become totally worthless in a very short time because of the inflation in Germany. At the end of eight months, the postal stamp for his last letter home cost two billion German marks!

Lajos was grateful to be able to study in Halle. The theological faculty of the Martin Luther University of Halle/Wittenberg, as it was called then and now, had a good reputation among Hungarian theologians. Already at the time of the Reformation, students from Hungary had studied with Luther and Melanchthon in Wittenberg. Moreover, there had been numerous Hungarian students in Halle. And there was even a copious Hungarian library, although it did not have the latest publications. The faculty consisted of internationally known theologians, without exception. There were the old liberals, Hermann Gunkel and his younger colleague and former student Otto Eissfeld, whose publications broke new ground in the field of Old Testament studies. The "conservative Ritschlian" Friedrich Loofs, who by this time had taught in Halle for thirty-five years, and the New Testament professor, Paul Feine, were well known, and not only in Hungary. In addition, there was Ernst von Dobschütz, who arrived during Lajos's first year and had begun work on the new edition of Nestle's Greek New Testament. Two professors had recently moved to Halle: the systematic theologian Horst Stephan and the church historian Johannes Ficker.

Ordass soon developed a good relationship with these last two. Stephan had published his book *Luther in the Changes of His Church (Luther in den Wandlungen seiner Kirche)* a few years earlier. Ficker worked on the publication of Luther's lecture manuscripts, which had just been discovered in the Vatican Library. These were stimulating themes for a young student who was especially interested in church history. He had long conversations with Stephan and was invited to Ficker's home.

During this time Lajos finally had the opportunity to devote himself completely to studying without having to earn his keep at the same time. He could even afford to visit some of the well-known sites of the Reformation. With other students he traveled to Eisenach and to the Wartburg. He was in Wittenberg on Reformation Sunday and attended the service at the Castle Church. Then he visited various museums and toured historical buildings in town. For the first time he could devote himself to study and travel without any worries.

But this happy time would not last. His secure stipend was devoured overnight by inflation. At Christmas time he stood in line for work at the student employment office. He hoped to earn enough within a few weeks to finance the rest of the academic year. But this was not to be. First he was assigned to work in a saltpeter mine not far from Halle. He was used to hard physical labor, but a bad diet and long working days depleted his energy. After a while, he had to look for other work. This time he ended up at a building site. The mining company built homes for laborers. He had to help with excavation and transport soil in a wheelbarrow. At least it was no longer underground work and he could breathe fresh air. But his hope for intensive theological study had changed into a race with time: from early morning, when he went to work, until the reading rooms closed in the evening.

Toward the end of the academic year 1922/23 he tried to get a visa for Yugoslavia. His attempts to do so in Hungary had failed. But the Yugoslavian embassy in Berlin was more generous. After a brief stay in Budapest, he was able to return home to Torzsa for the first time in five years. Much had happened in the family during these years. The two brothers had married, and one already had a daughter. Some members of the family had died. Sister Ilona had died after a few years of marriage. Shortly thereafter, her husband, a Lutheran pastor near Torzsa, also died. Sister Paula had also lost her husband, who had been one of Lajos's violin teachers. He was buried in Russia, along with many other Hungarian prisoners of war. Lajos had heard indirectly about some of these deaths during his time away from his family.

But this first encounter with his family after five years was marked by the joy of reunion as well as by mourning. There was great joy in the family to have a son and brother back again. They pampered him as much as possible. He was able to exchange his mended suits for new ones. The light overcoat was replaced by a specially ordered heavier one. He finally got shoes that fit. Not only did friends and acquaintances stare when they saw him at the beginning of the semester; he could hardly recognize himself in the mirror.

Lajos did not return to Budapest at the end of his studies in Germany, for the decision had been made to transfer the "fled" theological academies to Sopron (Ödenburg) and to merge them with the academy there. The new institution was to be elevated to the rank of a university faculty. Lajos went to the frontier town Sopron at the beginning of the semester, joined by thirty to forty other students. During vacation time his father had made arrangements with a bank so that the final year of Lajos's study was financially secured. Lajos no longer needed to live in one of the dormitories; instead, he rented his own room in town. He had never before been in Sopron. He found the mood a bit cool, in town as well as in the school. Much later he and his fellow students from Budapest learned that the Sopron students had heard rumors that the newcomers were liberal and disbelieving. It took some time to change this mood. At one point there was discussion regarding the founding of a student association. The dean had the delicate task of negotiating with the groups from Sopron and from Budapest about candidates to be in the executive committee. He must have been surprised when the students chose Lajos as their candidate even though he was from Budapest.

The kind Professor Deák and his colleague, the church historian Sándor Kovács, had come along to Sopron from Budapest. The majority of the teachers were well-established professors from Sopron. A new addition was Károly Karner. Later he would become one of the internationally best-known Hungarian theologians. Before he was forced to retire during the "purification" after the uprising in 1956, he had written a significant number of books and essays in the field of New Testament studies. He also authored other things as one who was engaged in a stirring struggle against the National-Socialist ideas in the Lutheran Church.

During his last year of study Lajos was invited to spend the Christmas vacation with one of his best friends, his fellow student Gusztáv Kirner. Kirner had a younger sister with whom Ordass became acquainted during this vacation time. Five years later, Irén Kirner would become his wife.

The last half year in Sopron passed quickly. Final examinations were close. With the assistance of Professor Deák, students revived the old tradition of visiting Lutheran congregations in groups in order to substitute as preachers and to organize evening meetings. Lajos and his friend Kirner exhibited a truly ardent zeal in these matters. These contacts strengthened their conviction that they were called to be parish pastors. Both had no doubt: after the examinations they would go directly into the parish. They would have liked best to take over one of these "diaspora congregations," which were so numerous in the Lutheran Church in Hungary. A "supply visit" in Nyiregyháza in eastern Hungary especially opened their eyes to the importance of such a service.

Lutherans comprised only 5 percent of the population in Hungary, and they were dispersed over almost the whole country. The Reformation of the sixteenth century had touched the whole region. Luther's teaching was so effective that by the end of the sixteenth century only 10 percent of the population remained loyal to the Catholic Church, according to official church records. But just as fast as the Reformation had gained a foothold, the Counter-Reformation succeeded in re-Catholicizing the country. Hungary was "purified from heresy" by every means, ranging from promises to threats, including prison sentences. During the reign of Empress Maria Theresa in the eighteenth century, the religious scene evolved that would endure until the years between two World Wars: about two-thirds Roman Catholic, 20 percent Reformed (Calvinists), and 5 percent Lutheran. There were some larger Lutheran groupings in the southern parts of the country and in the triangle between the Danube and Drau rivers in the west. But the majority of the 450,000 Lutherans lived dispersed in a series of larger and smaller towns and villages. Records from the time of the beginning of World War II list quite a few congregations comprising twenty to twenty-five locations in which there were only a few Lutherans. In one case there were more than one hundred such locations, once even one hundred and fifty. Given the number of congregations at that time, it was impossible to find enough pastors for the kind of effective service needed in the church.

Lajos and Kirner were quite impressed by their visits to scattered congregations and were deeply concerned about the problems of congregational dispersion. If young pastors with initiative could not stem the tide, these congregations would die. The two friends were also able to inspire Lajos's brother János for the cause during a vacation in Torzsa. He wanted to finance out of his own pocket one year of service for his brother, if he were called to such service. Lajos wrote a letter to Bishop Geduly in eastern Hungary and volunteered. But the answer was negative. No reason was given. But perhaps the bishop felt that the church needed young pastors to fill vacancies and therefore could not afford the kind of experiments suggested by Lajos.

Shortly thereafter Lajos was sent to the large Lutheran congregation in Harta on the Danube as a vicar. Harta was part of his home diocese. It was located about halfway between Budapest and the Yugoslavian border. The ordination was scheduled for October 5, 1924. Four other candidates were to be ordained at the same time in the main church in Deák-tér in Budapest. Lajos was to deliver the sermon since it was customary for a candidate to do so.

The evening before the ordination there was the traditional "first examination" before a commission existing of four members, presided over by the bishop. The bishop's final question was: "Did you study the sermon with care?" Ordass could answer yes with a good conscience. But the bishop was not satisfied. "Did you study it so well that you will be able to preach even if a woman passes out right under the pulpit?" Ordass was reminded of his past failures to recite poems at school celebrations. He could only respond: "Experience has to show." This was an honest answer. Then it happened the next day: during his sermon a woman passed out and was carried out of the church. Now he was happy about the bishop's final question the evening before. He had been prepared for this event, too.

During the final days before ordination he eagerly awaited his gown, which had been ordered well in advance. But it did not arrive in time. Finally, the bishop himself helped by lending Lajos his second gown. He did so with the words, "Take it. Who knows whether you might become bishop." This was the second utterance of Bishop Raffay about his successor.

After the ordination service, Ordass was saddened by the fact that all the other ordinands were surrounded by the cheerful, smiling faces of parents and siblings. He was once again alone.

7. A Year in Sweden

THREE YEARS of rich experience as a vicar followed Lajos's ordination. In the Lutheran Church in Hungary, the bishop places vicars as they may be required. When vicars have passed the "second examination" (two years after ordination at the earliest), they may be called by a congregation for regular service. In the course of his first three years of service Lajos had three such calls.

Quite often older pastors burdened their young vicars with so many tasks that they groaned under the inhuman load of work. At one location, where Lajos also had to serve, a vicar fled by night in order to escape from his very strict superior. Lajos had no reason to complain about such an overload in his first two assignments. In Harta, where he was a vicar for one and a half years, there were 1,600 members in the congregation; in Mezőberény, a center of agriculture, there were 4,000. In that location there were two Lutheran congregations, so Lajos was able to negotiate the amount of work with his colleagues so that he had time to read theological literature and to learn Swedish on his own. He also became a member of the string quartet in Mezőberény, and he had close contact with his friend and future brother-in-law Gusztáv Kirner, who had been called to the neighboring town Békéscsaba, about fifteen miles away.

His work schedule became tighter when he was assigned as vicar to Bishop Raffay. According to church polity, the bishop was simultaneously first pastor at the main congregation in Budapest. Here Lajos faced the tasks of serving a large city congregation, called to do preaching, youth work, and numerous home visitations. Moreover, the bishop did not hesitate to use the expertise of his vicar in shorthand and typing.

In addition, Lajos had to supply frequently in vacant neighboring congregations. The work here was more exacting and took more time, but he was better paid than before. In previous years the postwar inflation had stopped in Hungary, so Lajos was able to replace his wardrobe and lay the foundation for what was to become a large private library.

He had long dreamed of study in Sweden. Like many of his younger colleagues, he was attracted to the prospect of getting to know the great Scandinavian folk churches and being inspired by their rich theological and liturgical heritage. An opportunity to study there would also allow him to become acquainted with the influence of the great revival movements that had been quite strong in the north in the nineteenth century. After many unsuccessful attempts, Lajos finally in the fall of 1927 found an opportunity to study in Sweden. Together with a friend and colleague who had received a stipend for Finland, he traveled to Berlin. When they separated they agreed to exchange their experiences through diligent correspondence. This friend who traveled to Finland, Gyula Dedinszky, would later become the father-in-law of one of Lajos's daughters.

The journey to Sweden was quite an experience for a Hungarian who had never seen the ocean. He was to stay for one semester in Lund and a second in Uppsala. Thanks to his previous study of the Swedish language, it did not take long until he was able to understand the lectures and to read Swedish theological literature. Theological scholarship was then in its prime in Sweden. He attended lectures by Gustaf Aulén and Anders Nygren, and under the guidance of the expert church historian Hjalmar Holmquist he began to do research himself.

His project dealt with a time when significant political connections had existed between Hungary and Sweden, a time that was also important for Protestants in Hungary. The Swedish king, Gustavus Adolfus II (1594-1632), and his contemporary, the Hungarian duke of Siebenburgen, Gábor Bethlen (1580-1629), had corresponded with each other for some time. Bethlen became the leader of an armed rebellion against Hapsburg with the goal of securing religious freedom for Protestants. Lajos's research project dealt with this segment of church history. It also gave him an opportunity to become familiar with Scandinavian church history. He discovered much unknown material in libraries.

Just as significant for Lajos as the study at both universities was his experience of church life and his opportunities to meet many people who were very influential in the church and in theology.

Among the revival movements in Sweden, "Schartauanism" made

a special impression on Lajos. This movement was started by Henrik Schartau, who had preached for many years in the cathedral of Lund. In Uppsala, Lajos became acquainted with "Rosenianism." Six weeks of his winter vacation he spent in the small town of Sigtuna at Lake Mälaren, located between Stockholm and Uppsala. There the director of the "young church" movement, Manfred Björkquist, had built his center. Lajos got to know him personally. When Björkquist became the first bishop of the newly established diocese of Stockholm fourteen years later, Lajos was able to write an extensive report in a church paper about this important figure of the Swedish Church.

Lajos admired the foreign mission of the Swedish Church, especially since he was a member of a minority church. His newly awakened interest in missions was further nourished by an encounter with Albert Schweitzer. Schweitzer visited Lund while Lajos was studying there. He gave an organ concert in the cathedral, described his mission work in Lambarene, Africa, in a fascinating presentation, and also gave a scholarly philosophical lecture.

The Swedish mission made such an enduring impression on Lajos that he was later strongly supportive of the mission work of his own Hungarian church. Slowly, the vision of the church of Jesus Christ as a worldwide community became a reality for him, and this vision accompanied him until he himself occupied a leading position in the Lutheran World Federation.

Lajos and his fellow students were also influenced by the far-reaching lectures of Archbishop Nathan Söderblom. In addition, a series of noted theologians and churchmen spoke from the pulpit of the cathedral and in the lecture halls of the university. In the winter of 1918/19, Bishop Raffay and another church leader from Hungary had made presentations about their church in Uppsala. Söderblom was so impressed by these presentations that he later proposed to hold the first Lutheran World Convention in Budapest. (It was held in Eisenach instead.) As Bishop Raffay's vicar, Lajos encountered some of the best-known church leaders of his time in Uppsala.

Among the guest lecturers in Uppsala was the noted Danish church historian Valdemar Ammundsen, whom Lajos came to know. At that time Lajos began to show interest in Grundtvig and the "folk high school" movement, which later made him an ardent advocate for such programs in Hungary. Other stipendists brought similar ideas from Finland, so that a similar school was founded in the later 1930s.

Söderblom also took notice of the young vicar from Hungary. He invited him to his home, introduced him to the inner circle after guest lectures, and even took him along on visitations. Thus Lajos was able to come to know church life in Sweden from within. During a trip, Söderblom sent a newspaper clipping to Bishop Raffay, showing the Swedish archbishop together with his young friend from Hungary.

Perhaps the most important result of Lajos's year of study in Sweden was the many bonds of friendship he formed with his Swedish fellow students. Bishop Rodhe in Lund and Archbishop Söderblom in Uppsala took it on themselves to have individual students care for their guest from Hungary. Thus Lajos got to know a number of persons who would play leading roles in the Swedish church just a few years later. Many of these friendships remained intact. In Lund, Martin Lindström, later bishop there, and Harry Johansson, later the director of Swedish church aid and a driving force in interchurch work, became his friends. In Uppsala he shared a table at the student refectory with Gunnar Hultgren, who later became archbishop; with Ivar Hylander, later bishop of Luleå; with Nils Karlström, later rector of the cathedral; and, most importantly, with Bo Giertz, later bishop of Göteborg and a noted writer.

Just two years after his first visit to Sweden, Lajos was able to return, this time as a delegate of the World Congress for Diaconical Work. It was an occasion to renew contact with his many Swedish friends. The bonds of friendship established at this time would outlast the hard years of World War II and prove to be of immense help during his later years of suffering.

Lajos did not arrive in Norway until twenty years later. But already during his first stay in the north he also focused on church life in Norway, and, after his return home, he began to translate church literature from Norwegian as well as from Swedish.

It was inevitable that the young theologian would be strongly impressed by the democratic society in Scandinavia. His homeland was so strongly shaped by feudalism and class distinctions that it had been called "a sociological museum in the Europe of the twentieth century." His landlord in Lund was a shoemaker — that is, he had a vocation that ranked quite low on the social scale in Hungary. But the home of the shoemaker Jeremiasson could be easily compared with a middle-class home in Hungary. What impressed Lajos most was the fact that Mr. Jeremiasson used the telephone as a matter of course, a technological innovation that was reserved for the upper class in Hungary during the 1920s.

The study year ended well when he and his friend Dedinszky visited each other in Sweden and Finland after their lively correspondence during the year. Together they then traveled toward Hungary, this time by train via the Baltic states, Poland, and Czechoslovakia. Both had become true friends of the countries and the churches of the North during their year of study.

8. A Congregation Flourishes

AFTER HIS return from Sweden, Lajos was first assigned to be vicar of the congregation in Soltvadkert, south of Budapest. Then Bishop Raffay took him back again to the main church at Deák-tér. Meanwhile he had reached the point at which he could receive a regular call, and he applied for a position as military chaplain, which he later called a mistake. He worked for about a year as military chaplain in Debrecen, but he found no favorable conditions there for his service. There was no interest in church or Christianity among the officers, and no one wanted to support him. The soldiers were ordered to go to church, but their officers stayed outside the church door, talking and smoking. The climate in the officers' mess, to which he belonged because of his military rank, was marked by an unbearable pride of place. The officers despised anyone ranked lower than themselves, and they made no effort to hide their contempt. Lajos found no opportunities to execute his spiritual office, except for the weekly "hour of the pastor." A change to another chaplaincy in Budapest brought some improvement. But he had already decided to leave this kind of work.

He was very relieved when, after a confidential conversation with Bishop Raffay, the bishop immediately assigned him another task, which was more to his liking and which afforded him many more opportunities for development. He learned much during this assignment for his later life. Designated as "mission pastor" — more like a kind of "inner mission" than outward evangelism — he substituted for shorter or longer periods of time for pastors who were ill or on leave, and he also worked to bring inspiration and new initiatives in the areas of confirmation instruction, evangelism, diaconical work, and so on. Between trips he served as assistant to the bishop.

This was the kind of work Lajos loved. He did it for about a year, traveling in all directions in the large church district. He came to know pastors and congregational situations. He became familiar with local problems and collected experiences for effective work in a congregation. The extensive diocese comprised almost half of Hungary and almost half of the Lutherans in the country. (The other half extended to three other dioceses.) Only when he himself became the bishop of the same church district fifteen years later did it become clear to him how much he had learned during this year.

His work as "mission pastor" came to an end when the church council in Cegléd, about fifty miles southeast of Budapest, issued a unanimous call for him to become their pastor. He was installed on June 14, 1931. Thus began the period that he would later call the happiest years of his life.

Lajos did not come alone to Cegléd. In the summer of 1929 he had married Irén Kirner, the sister of his fellow student. It was a double wedding, for Gusztáv Kirner married at the same time.

Already at the end of the previous century the obligatory civil wedding had been introduced in Hungary. Gusztáv Kirner and his bride lived in Békéscsaba and were married there in a civil ceremony. Lajos traveled to Apostag, where his future father-in-law was teacher and organist, in order to be wed there to his bride Irén in a civil ceremony. Afterward both couples traveled to Budapest, where the bishop blessed both marriages in the main church.

Irén became a strong helper of her husband. She ran the household and entertained the many guests from nearby and abroad who increasingly visited her home, either on business or socially. Her fine voice was an asset in the choir. She put aside her own interests in order to be available to her husband as co-worker and helper. When they moved to Cegléd, their first child Barnabás was already a year old. Then came three daughters, Sára, Zsuzsanna, and Erzsébet. The third child, a son, lived only a few hours.

In Cegléd, as everywhere in Hungary, the Lutheran congregation constituted only a small part of the population. Of about 40,000 inhabitants, only 1,112 were Lutheran. The Reformed, who comprised about 20 percent of the Hungarian population, were especially numerous in Cegéd, with 17,000 members, and had always shaped life in the city.

During the last generation, the Catholics had become the majority due to the influx of immigrants from the surrounding farming population.

In the years before Lajos's arrival, the Lutheran congregation of Cegléd had a solid financial foundation. As was the custom then, the congregation owned farmland whose yield was available for congregational support. In addition, the congregation owned real estate, the rents of which also contributed to the security of the congregational budget. A few years before the family arrived a splendid elementary school had been built without exacting any additional church tax from the members.

The Lutheran congregation in Cegléd played a larger role in public life than one might expect, given the number of members. In a number of elections Lutherans had supplied mayors. They were also well represented among gymnasium teachers and in other academic vocations.

Despite the congregation's past secure financial base, the economic misery of the 1930s had already begun to take its toll before Lajos arrived. Some of the larger businesses that had rented buildings owned by the congregation had to close, thus decreasing the church's income from renting. The number of unemployed increased daily. The mortgage of the newly built elementary school became a heavy burden for the congregation.

In addition, there had been unrest in the congregation for a number of years due to internal quarrels. Church attendance had decreased, and individual aspects of church work had been neglected. Thus there was plenty of work to do when the small family moved into the parsonage.

The weak financial situation of the congregation confronted the pastor with difficult tasks. But it seemed even more important to him to address the internal situation. The children's service on Sunday was one of his first innovations. Attendance increased steadily. Lajos sought help from Scandinavian friends for this challenging work. He received books of worship and collections of sermons that he used in the children's services. After the service he "tested" the children by referring to the content during religious instruction. The children's sermons written by the Norwegian "children's bishop" Johan Lunde proved to be most helpful. Lajos translated two volumes. They were published with a preface by Bishop Lunde and were sold out in a short time. His colleagues in the ministry used both volumes and praised them. Encouraged by such positive reaction, he asked his friend Dedinszky to translate a selection of Finnish children's services and sermons. A younger colleague, who had been a stipendist after him in Sweden, translated some Swedish books of children's services. Lajos occupied himself with the Norwegian and Danish literature in this field, publishing an impressive two-volume work entitled *The Children's Sunday*.

The Lutheran students were dispersed in several schools of the town. In the elementary schools the teachers of various denominations provided the religious instruction for the children of their own denomination. At the gymnasium, in the civic school, in the vocational schools, and in all other schools, religious instruction was the task of the pastor. With the cooperation of the various school administrations, Lajos was able to assemble students from several grades and even from different schools for a combined religious instruction class. But he still had to teach sixteen hours each week, in addition to the confirmation instruction. He also succeeded in putting together a youth group in his congregation. In the beginning, the youth group consisted of two girls and one boy, and it met in one classroom of the new elementary school. Later he was able to use rooms in one of the congregation's business buildings in the center of town that was no longer being rented. The young people fixed the rooms up, together with the Lutheran students from the vocational school. There was even a small workshop where toys and other handicraft were produced to be given as gifts at the Christmas celebration.

For many years Lajos had been interested in doing diaspora work in communities that had only a few Lutherans. Now he could translate his commitment into practice. In his parish there were many little towns and villages where only a few Lutheran members lived. The neighboring town, Abony, ten miles from Cegléd, listed eight Lutherans in a record left by Lajos's predecessor. After his first visit to the town, the number doubled. His regular visits discovered more and more Lutherans so that after a few years there were about a hundred. Finally, a church council was established in Abony and an altar was erected in a classroom of the civic school. During the week it was kept hidden behind a curtain. A small organ was bought, and on the first Sunday of every month a worship service was conducted in the afternoon.

The Abony group became the largest group among the groups in the Cegléd diaspora. In addition, there were six to eight locations that were so far away from the church that worship services had to be conducted in homes or schools there. But there was not enough time on Sunday! Youth and children's programs were also conducted on Sunday in Cegléd. In addition, there was Holy Communion every Sunday, which was attracting more and more people. The pastor had to care for the distant locations during the week. Through systematic and solid preparation and with the help of people on location he succeeded in bringing the dispersed Lutherans to these weekly events, followed by religious instruction of children who came regularly.

The bicycle or walking were the pastor's usual means of transportation in diaspora work. A village five miles away had fourteen members. The pastor usually went there on foot because the road was too bad for a bicycle. When his wife asked him afterward how many had assembled, he usually answered: "I walked one kilometer (about two-thirds of a mile) for every one." That meant that all fourteen had attended!

Such intensive work in the diaspora radiated back to the main congregation. In a stirring meeting four years after Lajos's arrival, the thirty members of the church council took the initiative to collect additional church taxes in order to further a more intensive work among dispersed Lutherans. At the same time, they prepared the way for a second pastor. They understood that the pastor was burning his light on both ends of the candle.

There was a steady increase in worship attendance. More and more members volunteered for work in the congregation. Lajos was rarely alone on his trips to the diaspora. At one time members of the council would go, at another time a whole group of young folk. The members of the congregation embellished the simple services, both in the diapora churches and in the main church, with song and music, and they themselves were grateful for their fellowship with the pastor. He was always able to tell them about interesting things, especially about his trips abroad and his contact with fellow Christians in the faraway north, which seemed exotic to them.

Lajos, who had had such great difficulties with public appearances in his school days, enjoyed preaching more and more. Preaching was no longer a burden but a task he did joyfully, with deeper insights and greater personal understanding of the biblical message. Even when he was a military chaplain and had a Sunday off from preaching, he preferred to substitute in a congregation where there would not have been a service otherwise. As long as there were open pulpits, preaching was for him a priority.

Finally it really became necessary to call a vicar. It was good for

Lajos that after five years as the only pastor in the congregation he could now let a vicar be responsible for youth work and religious instruction. One of the vicars who served with him in Cegléd was György Kendeh, a solid, conscientious co-worker on whom Lajos could rely. He also became a close friend who never deserted him, not even during the later stormy times when friendship with Lajos could have unpleasant consequences.

Encouraged by Lajos, there were for the first time conventions for church councils in Hungary for the exchange of experiences and for mutual inspiration. The bishop was the main speaker at the first convention in 1933. The feedback was so positive that the conventions were repeated annually in different congregations. Another new initiative was the "congregation days," when pastors and laypeople assembled from the neighboring congregations to focus on worship, evangelism, visitation, and programs for children and young adults. Such events had a great effect in motivating congregations and in gaining volunteers.

The economic crisis of the 1930s had a growing impact on Cegléd. Many suffered financially, indeed some were in dire need. But a feeling of common responsibility grew with the difficulties. When Lajos visited the dispersed congregations at Christmas time, his bags were filled with shoes, clothes, and toys, gifts collected by the congregation. But the congregation's compassion was not limited to a single action. During the most difficult years the congregation fed twenty-five students of the congregation who were in great need with a hot meal every day.

The local pastor also had other obligations. Lajos was a member of the town council, the vice president of the school board, and the president of the commission for the kindergarten. At one time he had hoped to pursue doctoral studies, but he had to drop that plan. He also had to give some time to his family. The family visited their relations in Torzsa and even spent some vacation time at the Adriatic Sea.

After six years in Cegléd, on the day when his daughter Zsuzsanna was born, he was informed that he had been elected "senior" of the "middle-Pest" district. This office was not connected with ministry in a particular congregation. Lajos could stay in Cegléd, but he would have two vicars, because the new position involved many obligations. Later he would look back with joy at two initiatives he had taken as senior. First, he had produced a solid record of the various diaspora groups and secured regular service for them through the district's creation of a special office for diaspora ministry. Second, he had gained a printing press for the district. A printing press had rented rooms from the congregation. When one of the owners fell ill, the other owner looked for a new partner. Lajos persuaded some members of the congregation to put up the money so that the district could be a partner. The young and reliable printer developed the business into a growing enterprise that steadily received orders from places throughout the whole country. The printing press was modernized, and business expanded so that the profit was sufficient not only to repay loans but also to contribute to the salary of the diaspora pastor.

In 1931 Lajos had taken charge of a congregation that was in a critical situation, both spiritually and materially. When he left it ten years later, he entrusted a flourishing congregation to his successor. But at that time the world was already on fire.

9. War Years in Budapest

GRADUALLY THE active and energetic pastor and "senior" in Cegléd received more and more notice. He was frequently invited to speak at evening assemblies of congregations and at conventions. He became a member of the committee for examination in practical theology. He was given leading roles and became president of the league of Lutheran pastors in the church district. He was sent to church gymnasiums to preside at the commission for examinations.

Various feelers had been sent out, when larger calls in Budapest or elsewhere were available, to find out whether the senior of Cegléd might be willing to change his position. For a long time Lajos flatly refused such offers. But when in the early summer of 1941 a large delegation from the congregation at Kelenföld in Budapest told him that the council had called him unanimously as pastor, Lajos accepted. He knew that there was much good behind the call. Sándor Kovács, who had been his professor of church history and who later became bishop in a neighboring diocese, was his advocate in Kelenföld. Ever since school, he had shown a lively interest in the fate of his student.

With five hundred members, Kelenföld was one of the largest Lutheran congregations among the sixteen in the capital. The situation here was much better than the one he had encountered earlier in Cegléd. The congregation had been separated in 1924 from a larger congregation and was therefore relatively young. The membership was constantly growing, and it owned a splendid sanctuary surrounded by offices and rooms for congregational activities as well as homes for church workers. Attendance in church was very good, and active laypeople supported a series of enterprises. A local Lutheran academy was responsible for lectures and printing, drawing the attention of the whole Lutheran Church. On the whole, Kelenföld was known as a model congregation. Besides the senior pastor, there was a special position for religious instructor in the schools, and there was also a vicar.

Such a congregation naturally had its long-range plans. There had been much talk about transferring the well-known Lutheran gymnasium for girls from the cramped rooms at the main church at Deák-tér to another location in the capital. The Kelenföld congregation wanted to supply new facilities and to provide a boarding school for students from the whole country. There were also plans to build a Lutheran elementary school and a kindergarten. But it did not take long for the congregation to discover that this was no time for expansion, indeed, that much of what already existed had to be given up.

When Lajos was installed on November 2, 1941, Hungary had not yet felt the worst consequences of the war. Amazingly, politicians had succeeded in steering the country through the threatening storms that had invaded neighboring lands. National independence was still preserved. But the country's geographical location would soon bring about unavoidable consequences.

After 1938, three laws had been accepted under pressure from National-Socialist Germany that severely limited the freedom of movement for Jews. The media had been coordinated, and a special police force watched everyone who had been labeled a "Communist." People who had a clearly democratic stance were also called "Communists." The appointed administrator Admiral Horthy and his government still had power. The "arrow crosses" party, which would later become notorious, held a minority of less than 10 percent in the parliament at this time; the Social Democrats were still represented until 1943.

In April 1941, Hitler used Hungary for his invasion of Yugoslavia. The prime minister of Hungary committed suicide because the agreement of friendship he had made with Yugoslavia had become a useless piece of paper. In the summer of 1941 Hungary was also drawn into the war against the Soviet Union.

In the fall of 1942 the first two bombing raids took place in the Hungarian capital. After this events moved quickly, and Hungary was formally occupied by Germany in March of 1944. Five months later, the first Soviet troops arrived in the land, which then became a battlefield until April 1945.

The fate of the church became a very personal matter for Lajos after his move to Budapest. The aging bishop Raffay gave him special tasks. Now and then Lajos felt compelled to take his own initiatives without asking for either permission or advice.

After the Germans had marched into Yugoslavia, the regions that had been lost after World War I were once again under Hungarian administration. Torzsa, Lajos's hometown, was among these regions. Lajos of course made contact with his family. He was glad that his relatives could come to his installation in Kelenföld, since they had not been able to come to his ordination, his wedding, his previous installations, or his children's baptisms. But at the same time he was made uneasy by his contact with the Batschka region. He observed with growing apprehension how the "great-German" propaganda was increasingly gaining a foothold among those of German descent.

Leaders in the German-speaking congregations presented a "memorandum" to the administration of the Lutheran Church, making certain claims. On the surface it looked as if they wanted more self-determination. But at the same time they wanted to create closer ties with the German "folk league," an organization dominated by National-Socialists. The memorandum clearly indicated their distance from the "Confessing Church" in Germany, even though there was a certain critique of the "German Christians." The church administration tried to draw the matter out for fear of political complications.

Lajos clearly detected the National-Socialist agitation, with its ideological overtones, that was shaping the continual demands of congregations of German descent. He offered counterproposals that were partly heeded by church administrators. But in the end he realized that the position of the church administration was too cautious. So he chose to attack by publishing a "Response" to the memorandum in the spring of 1942. He also contributed to the clarification of the ideological front lines with articles in journals; the first of these was published in the Lutheran magazine *Christian Truth (Keresztyén Igazság)*, which he edited together with Károly Karner. Lajos was surprised that he was not called to account about his positions and writings, for he openly criticized the "folk league" and the official church administration in Berlin. It is possible that neither the police nor politicians found time to busy themselves with his case.

He regularly listened to Swedish radio broadcasts, which, among other things, also commented continuously on the church struggle in

Norway. Reading a Swedish magazine, Lajos learned that one of his teachers in Lund, Gustav Aulén, the bishop of Strängnäs, had done a presentation on the Norwegian church struggle; it had also appeared in print. He was able to get the Aulén article from the Swedish embassy in Budapest with the help of mail by diplomatic courier. He translated the article as quickly as possible into Hungarian and sent the manuscript to the four Hungarian bishops and to the theological faculty. He also used this material for a presentation at clergy convocations in several seniorial territories. This was a courageous move in the winter of 1942/43, even in the closed circles of clergy and laity. The now coordinated media had offered quite a different view of the situation in Norway. The presentation drew attention and caused repeated discussions in the Lutheran Church. Fortunately, this action, too, did not have troublesome consequences for Lajos.

There never was a public church struggle in Hungary. Since the government was able to delay a direct German occupation, the Hungarian National-Socialists had neither the opportunity to develop comprehensive ideological programs nor the power to realize them. But when they forcefully came to power on October 15, 1944, the Soviet army was already positioned at the Danube in Southern Hungary. The Nazis had too many other difficulties to begin a church struggle.

In the midst of this ever-growing tension Lajos moved to an even more dangerous field: helping Jews. The two "Jew laws" of 1938/39 were not as radical as the corresponding laws in Nazi Germany. But the third "Jew law," which had been passed by the Hungarian parliament already in the summer of 1941, was unequivocally racist. Church leaders who were then members of the Upper House sharply criticized it. After the formal occupation in the spring of 1944, the Germans took the "final solution" into their own hands, unfortunately with active support from Hungarians. But the situation of Jews became very critical after the coup d'état of the Nazis in October 1944.

Lajos had continual contact with the delegate of the Swedish Red Cross, Valdemar Langlet. The Swedish embassy had asked Lajos on occasion to do Swedish pastoral acts for Swedes in Hungary during his stay at Cegléd. He became a friend of Langlet. It was commonly known that diplomats of neutral countries worked untiringly for the persecuted Jews. The Swede Raoul Wallenberg and the Swiss Carl Lutz probably saved the lives of tens of thousands of Jews. Langlet's actions were not as compehensive, but of equal quality. He also distributed Swedish "protection passes," a document that had no legal value but was accepted in practice by the police and the Nazis. The Hungarian police were often glad to find an excuse not to have to arrest Jews. Lajos worked with Langlet and received Swedish protection passes from him. He once even succeeded in obtaining a regular Swedish passport for a persecuted Jew and thus helped him to emigrate to Sweden.

Together with Langlet, Lajos traveled to the head of the Roman Catholic Church, Cardinal Jusztinián Serédi, who resided in Esztergom. Lajos came with the power of attorney from his own ill bishop Raffay and from the Reformed bishop László Ravasz. There was to be a common declaration of the Christian churches in Hungary regarding the Jewish question. Langlet reports about it in his book *Work and Days in Budapest (Verk och dagar i Budapest)*, which was published in Stockholm immediately after the war. Unfortunately, this attempt to create a common stance failed because the distance between the churches was too great. The cardinal gave an evasive answer and decided, after the meeting, to protest only in the name of his own church. The Protestants then could also on their part only do so in their own name. Lajos continued his work with Langlet until it became impossible to move in the streets because of the war.

Lajos also had close contact with the Norwegian missionary Gisle Johnson, who led the Norwegian Israel Mission in Budapest from 1922 until his death in 1946. Johnson kept his distance from the clergy of the Hungarian Lutheran Church, but he got on well with Lajos. They became friends, and before he died he asked Lajos to celebrate Holy Communion and to bury him.

On the very day when Germany occupied Hungary, Lajos made the application to change his name Wolf to Ordass ("wolf" in Hungarian). From that point on he avoided the name Wolf. His request was granted seven months later.

Lajos Ordass also hid many of those who were politically persecuted during the reign of terror of the Hungarian National-Socialists after October 15, 1944. A government official who played a leading role in the resistance movement was able to stay for some time in the Kelenföld parsonage. From there he was taken out of Hungary, with help from Budapest. A year and a half earlier, the Hungarian Department of State had asked Ordass whether he wanted to live for a few years in Stockholm. He was to take the position of embassy pastor with diplomatic authority. The Hungarian side hoped for a separate peace treaty with the Allies and wanted to strengthen diplomatic relations with neutral countries in order to gain a basis for negotiations with London and Moscow. Ordass expressed his willingness for a brief stay, but the matter fell into oblivion because of the increasingly chaotic situation.

Ordass did not tell much about this time. He did not want to join the chorus of those who boasted about their deeds during the war and the Nazi period.

On December 17, 1944, Irén Ordass was taken to a hospital because of an acute attack of asthma. A week later the Red Army encircled Budapest so that there was no longer any communication between the various parts of the city. The hospital was located on the Soviet side of the front, while Kelenföld was taken by the Red Army only in February. In the meantime, Ordass had no contact with his wife.

The battle for Budapest lasted seven weeks. The Soviet troops advanced street by street. After four weeks all of Pest — that is, the eastern bank of the Danube — was in Russian hands. In Buda, where Kelenföld was located, the battle lasted three more weeks. Five Danube bridges were blown up when German troops retreated to the western bank. The nine-hundred-foot-long Margaret bridge had been destroyed already on November 4, when the dynamite charges under the bridge were ignited by mistake. It happened during rush-hour traffic so that three fully occupied street cars and hundreds of pedestrians fell into the river. An estimated three hundred to six hundred people perished.

During the battle, the population lived in underground shelters and cellars. On the day after Christmas the supply of electricity ceased until May 24. There was no supply of water from January 2 until the beginning of March.

The parsonage in Kelenföld was so severely damaged on the day after Christmas that no one could stay there. There was a rain of shells and bombs. The shelter, which had been built under the church steeple, was designed to hold fifteen to twenty people for a brief time. But now it had to serve as living quarters for thirty people for seven weeks, among whom were ten elderly women from the home for old people maintained by the congregation.

The biggest problem in the shelter was obtaining the supplies needed for daily living. The elderly women had no reserves of food. Neither the pastor nor his vicar nor the sacristan had counted on a siege of seven weeks. Many people starved to death during this time. The inhabitants of the shelter under the church in Kelenföld grew noticeably thinner, but survived.

Fortunately, there was snow and rain during these weeks. This helped the supply of water. In addition, the men dug a well in the garden, but the water had to be filtered and boiled before it could be consumed. The sacristan had saved stumps of altar candles for years. Now they could be used.

There was no way of doing work in the church. Certain streets were constantly under fire. It would have been suicidal to cross them. One of the inhabitants of the shelter was struck by a bullet. It was not a severe wound, but since it could not be treated correctly the wounded person died after a few weeks. At certain times of day, however, it was possible to move about safely. People knew where the Lutheran pastor was. He was also called by members of other churches for baptisms, Holy Communions, visitation of the sick, or burial of the dead in gardens and parks. He conducted Bible studies in nearby shelters and also worship services at festival days, and there were daily devotions in the shelter under the church steeple.

Ordass still found time for his academic work. In the winter of 1942/43 he had taken some books he had just received from Sweden into the shelter during the first air raids on Budapest. One of the books, *And Some Fell on the Rocks,* authored by his friend Bo Giertz, had so fascinated him that he not only immediately read it but also began translating it into Hungarian. This translation was published in the spring of 1943, in the midst of the war, by the publishing house of the Lutheran Church in Budapest.

During the final phase of the war he took plays written by the Danish martyr, pastor, and poet Kaj Munk with him into the shelter. He was able to translate four of them during the battle of Budapest: *He Is Sitting at the Melting Pot, The Victor, An Idealist,* and *The Word.* While translating, he read the texts aloud to his fellow lodgers in the shelter. But his translations of the plays were published only thirty years later, in Denmark.

On February 11, the first Soviet soldier appeared in the shelter under the church steeple. One week later, the last German soldier surrendered in the cellar of the once splendid but now totally destroyed imperial castle.

One day later Mrs. Ordass came home from the hospital, still ill and exhausted, dragging her things in a bundle behind her.

10. Bishop in Hard Times

THE PARSONAGE in Kelenföld was in a sad state. Only one room, Ordass's study, could be sufficiently repaired to make it habitable; it had only one window, which could be filled up with pieces of glass from other windows and with boards to keep out the worst of the cold.

The church did not have any windows either. Volunteers from the congregation removed the rubble from the church. The first worship service was held on February 18, 1945, the first Sunday in Lent, one week after the Red Army had occupied Kelenföld. A sizable congregation gathered in the cold, windowless church. People had come through the city ruins to the church to give thanks for having survived the siege.

The weeks of suffering in shelters and cellars had left visible traces. Most of those who attended that first church service had aged beyond their years. Only a few families had survived without losses. Many had died during the battles. Even more died afterward. The totally exhausted people fell victim to cold, lack of food, or psychological stress. Lack of supplies created a very critical situation in the capital. Whoever could move from the city to relatives and friends in the country did so. There were still some reserves there.

The Ordass children were sent to friends in Békéscsaba. Mrs. Ordass was in such a critical state of health that she needed to be hospitalized once more. As soon as a pontoon bridge had been built across the Danube in the middle of March, Ordass took his sick wife to Pest, in a handcart borrowed from the fire brigade, for a hospital bed was available only in Pest.

The beautiful city at the Danube had been transformed into a sea of ruins. In some parts of the city there were only a few houses left. In the part called Várhegy, bordering on Kelenföld, only four houses out of eight hundred were still intact. In the center on the Pest side there were thirty-five houses out of five hundred and twenty-eight.

The Red Army viewed Hungary as enemy territory. Soldiers plundered for three days and took from the civilian population whatever they wanted. Watches were the most wanted items. But the most incredible things were stolen from homes or from those who had valuable items with them in the street. And whatever valuables were left soon changed owners in the constant struggle to get food and fuel. The Hungarian money, the Pengö, lost its value very quickly.

The congregation in Kelenföld was able to restore its church in a short time. An elderly couple had bequeathed a villa to the Catholic and the Lutheran congregations in Kelenföld. Almost miraculously, the congregations were able to sell the villa for hard currency, despite the existing chaotic conditions. The Lutheran congregation used the proceeds to renovate the church. Due to the loyalty and support of many members, the church was ready for use again in October. Even the stained-glass windows had been restored. It was probably the first church in Budapest to be restored so quickly. The neighboring Catholic congregation completed work on its church only nine years later.

Life began again only very slowly after the long siege. One rather hopeless task facing the pastor in the starved and ruined city was that of burying the dead. A funeral could become a time-consuming and complex undertaking. Telephone and public transportation did not work. When the pastor arrived at the cemetery, after a tiring hike, he often found that the grave had not been dug or that the relatives of the deceased had not arrived. When the mourning family finally arrived, transporting the deceased in a box or locker, the tools for digging had to be procured in order to dig the grave. At times, the necessary tools had to be obtained from another family who also faced the same task of burying a relative, so they had to be helped first. But neither the pastor nor the families were in the best physical condition to do such work; they also were not used to it. In addition, the ground was frozen in the spring. Thus a funeral might take a whole workday, with just enough time left for a few home visits on the long way back on foot.

During the last years of the war there was repeated talk about the wish of the aging Bishop Sándor Raffay to retire. But he would not risk a change of leadership in the church during this critical situation. So he stayed in office despite his old age and a painful paralysis; he did his task with an impressive sense of duty and commitment. Finally, on his seventy-ninth birthday in June of 1945, he announced his decision to retire.

Ordass had already been asked by members of the church administration whether he wanted to stand for election. Among others, the then campus pastor László Dezséry had asked him to do so. Later, Dezséry would become one of Ordass's worst enemies; he took over the office of bishop when Ordass was arrested. The president of the church council in Kelenföld, who was also a member of the central church council, belonged to those who supported Ordass's candidacy. Ordass reluctantly agreed, but he was convinced that another candidate, Senior Lajos Kemény, would be elected. But Ordass was elected with one hundred and twenty-four votes, while Kemény received only eighty-five. Some few had voted for other candidates; fifteen votes were invalid. Thus Ordass had an absolute majority of the vote. On September 27, 1945, he was installed in his office by Bishop Raffay at a worship service at Deák-tér.

One could rightly ask whether any Hungarian bishop began his office under such hopeless external conditions as Lajos Ordass faced. Half of the 450,000 Lutherans in Hungary belonged to his diocese. A majority lived in Budapest, which was virtually in ruins. But the problems and worries were not just caused by the material damage. The war had also thrown the country into a gigantic financial crisis. It was estimated that the retreating German army had succeeded in taking along one thousand railroad trains, each with fifty cars filled with food, medicine, machinery, coal, mineral oil, and other goods. Additional goods were taken on trucks and ships moving up the Danube. According to official reports, the Hungarian national railway had only a tenth of its locomotives and trains at the end of the war. The losses and devastation in other areas were just as great. The whole nation had become very poor, without any possibility for economic recovery.

The postwar years were also hard on Ordass's closest relatives. Mrs. Ordass gradually recovered. Now and then she was able to travel to friends in the country, where the food shortage was felt less than in Budapest. The bishop's two sisters, who had stayed in Yugoslavia, were detained, together with many others from the same district. They spent one year under the most difficult conditions. After many attempts to obtain permission to

BISHOP IN HARD TIMES

leave, they were finally allowed to do so through the assistance of the Hungarian Department of State. They arrived in Hungary in the fall of 1946, totally impoverished and in bad physical condition. They verified the rumor that Ordass's brother János as well as his brother-in-law, the teacher Böhm, had perished. The news had been kept secret until this time in order to spare the feelings of the family.

The family managed to move from the parsonage in Kelenföld to the bishop's residence on the other side of the Danube by means of a cart drawn by an emaciated horse which hardly yielded one horsepower. The pontoon bridge was in such precarious condition that the coachman and the bishop had to take turns pushing and braking in order to bring the cart undamaged to the other side. Naturally, the bishop could not pay for the move in cash because no one took on such work for money. Used children's clothes and even the excellent boots that had served the pastor of Cegléd so well on his long hikes in the diaspora congregation were used as pay.

The bishop's salary was hardly a dollar per month, given the exchange rate then. A vicar in the country earned more than his bishop because he received part of his payment in natural goods.

Several months after his installation, Ordass visited the congregation in Pilis, about twenty-five miles from Budapest. For half the distance he could ride a street car. Another six miles he traveled in an overcrowded bus without seats, and the rest of the way he was transported by a council member of the congregation in a horse carriage. The council member also took him back again to the bus on the next day. But the bus was already so overcrowded that he had to hike to the street car.

The inflation that was beginning was one of the worst in history. When Ordass went to visit the seminary in Sopron for two days, he took along double the amount of the billions he had to pay for the journey there. There were no round trip tickets at that time. When he went to buy a ticket for the return journey he found that the price of the ticket had increased five times in two days. The bishop had to borrow money in order to return to Budapest. Another time, when the connection was somewhat firm, the bishop sent a telegram to a congregation. Ten words cost so much that three employees in the bishop's office had to put up all their cash in order to send the telegram.

It was nearly impossible to administer a church district under such conditions. The numerous circular letters had to be typed out many times on the typewriter using carbon paper. The postage could be organized only with much effort. Almost the only way of keeping contacts with congregations was through people who happened to travel.

Gradually, the conditions became more normal. The government issued authorizations for buildings and material for them. There were subsidies for the renovation of schools, public buildings, and churches. But because of the unstable political situation, experts and officials were so often exchanged that it was almost impossible to complete one matter at one office. It was not unusual to obtain a promise from an official, only to find that the person was no longer in office a week later. It was a great relief when the sister churches abroad noticed the bad situation in the war-damaged countries of Europe and began their relief actions. From then on, the office of the bishop became the center of distribution of textiles, shoes, medicine, flour, oil, sugar, paper, window glass, and so on.

It is difficult to express in words the joy and enthusiasm brought about in the winter of 1946/47 by the help from the churches in Scandinavia, Switzerland, and the United States. First, of course, children received help. Locations were established where food was distributed especially to children. Moreover, the Red Cross and ecclesiastical organizations took children abroad for recuperation. Swedish organizations founded a "truck bridge" for continual transportation of medicine, food, and other goods. The World Council of Churches and the Lutheran World Federation sent representatives to Hungary in order to become informed about the situation. Since Ordass had his office in the capital, he was commissioned to organize whatever help was needed for the whole country.

Through this generous assistance people were saved from starvation and despair, and congregations were encouraged to help themselves. In some places congregational life had been virtually paralyzed; there was no motivation left. A shipment of window glass arrived in one such place to replace the church windows that had been destroyed in the war. Now volunteers from the congregation went to work. The windows were replaced. Such an event broke the paralyzing despondency and helped the whole church to begin again. One congregation received food and money in order to provide for fifty children for three months. Suddenly, the members of the congregation became "infected." They collected enough potatoes, flour, oil, and even money to provide for eighty children for five months. Similar examples abounded.

Ordass used to say often that help in the church always "multiplies" — that is, that one could again and again experience the miracle of the multiplication of the bread. He also said that in his experience the Christian church made more out of the gifts through frugality and imagination than did the "official" helping organizations.

With the agreement of the Swedish embassy, Ordass could house Swedish and Danish truck drivers in the Lutheran house for deaconesses in Budapest. The deaconesses exhibited an exemplary hospitality to the guests from the north. There were flowers in each room and a hand-painted little card with a Bible verse in the driver's mother tongue. Ordass himself conducted a brief worship service in Swedish every morning. The truck drivers, who frequently had no connection to the church, often made a detour to the house of deaconesses when they returned to their homeland in order to relate their experiences and return greetings.

Despite all the time required to mediate the growing help from abroad, Ordass continued to fulfill his duties as shepherd of his pastors and congregations as best he could in the difficult circumstances.

Gradually the situation in the country normalized. In the fall of 1946 a new currency was introduced that proved to be stable. Trains ran again, even according to schedule. Since Hungary was an agricultural country it was able to recuperate faster than some impoverished industrial countries.

Thus the bishop was soon able to exercise his office under more normal circumstances and more effectively. Before his arrest in August of 1948, Ordass succeeded in visiting all of the nearly one hundred congregations of the diocese, either on an official visitation, as pastor of the pastor, or as a guest at anniversaries and dedications of churches. He earned the trust of congregations through his clear proclamation and the objective manner in which he conducted negotiations. He was able to encourage many pastors through public speaking and theological advice; many pastors had lost their orientation in the difficult postwar situation. Ordass was respected within and without the church because of his solid stance in disputes.

There was no lack of conflict during the first years after the war. Protected by the power of Soviet military occupation, the country gradually moved in the direction of securing the most important positions in society for the Communist party. Such a change did not happen without conflict. Now and then Ordass had to interfere personally in order to help Lutheran pastors — at times successfully, but not always — who had gotten in trouble with the authorities or the media.

When one of the Lutheran pastors in Budapest, Károly Grünvalszky, was falsely accused of anti-Semitism in the official government newspaper, Ordass was ready to go to the very top in defense of him. But the Communist-controlled media were already so powerful that Grünvalszky regarded the intervention on his behalf as too dangerous. So Ordass reluctantly let the matter go.

Hatred of everything German was so strong that the German-speaking congregation in Budapest decided to dissolve. But Ordass was of the opinion that all Lutheran citizens in Hungary, including those who spoke German, had a right to have worship services in their mother tongue. When the pastor of the congregation refused to preach in German, Ordass himself took over. For several years he was the only one in Hungary who dared to hold Lutheran worship services in German.

He who had resisted German nationalism so energetically now strongly supported the perscuted German minority. Violating international law, the Hungarian authorities had decreed the expulsion of the German minority. The expulsion was effected at short notice. Only a minimum of possessions could be taken along. The expulsion affected a group of people who had lived in Hungary for three hundred years. These people who had stayed in the country after the war were mostly loyal citizens who had never done anything wrong. The Nazis among the German descendants had left the country already in the winter of 1944/45. Ordass's courageous opposition to this government action created respect for him in the church. But it also resulted in the Communist authorities becoming aware of him and viewing his actions with growing suspicion.

11. Travels

Toward the end of 1946, Ordass was asked to visit the president of the republic, Zoltán Tildy. The kingdom of Hungary, expecting the election of a new king during the time between the wars, was governed by a "governor," but was declared a republic in the summer of 1946. Three years later Hungary received a new constitution and was officially declared a "people's republic."

Zoltán Tildy was a Reformed pastor. He was made president in 1946 even though he had no particular political experience. A few years later, the real rulers of the land, the state security police, made available a dossier, according to which Tildy's son-in-law was involved in a conspiracy against the republic. So Tildy had to make a silent retreat. But even at the end of 1946 many Hungarians still hoped that he might be able to withstand the growing pressure of the Communists as a man of neutrality and integrity.

Tildy wanted to speak with Ordass about a report that had reached him from the Hungarian ambassador in Stockholm. The archbishop of Uppsala had hinted to the ambassador that he wanted to expand Swedish help for Hungary. But before taking any steps he wished to be informed about the situation in Hungary by the personal report of a representative of the Hungarian church.

Ordass told Tildy that he had tried for a year to get a passport. Already before Christmas 1945 he had received a personal invitation from the Swedish archbishop. Tildy assured Ordass that he would do what he could to have the passport application approved. It was characteristic of the situation in Hungary at that time that not even the president of the republic could promise a compatriot an exit permit. First, one had to get a passport from the ministry of the interior, which had been controlled since the end of the war by the Communist Party. Then the Russian military occupation authority had to issue a special exit permit. Anyone who left the country even for a day had to have such a permit, which was even more difficult to get than a passport.

After a few months and some effort, the bishop was in possession of both documents and enabled to travel. The next step was to arrange his trip. He had been invited to attend the annual assembly of the Committee of Relief and Reconstruction of the World Council of Churches in Switzerland, and afterward he would travel to Sweden. He also had an invitation to attend the constituting assembly of the Lutheran World Federation, which was meeting in Lund, but that would not take place until the end of June. It was not advisable to return to Hungary in between, since there was no assurance that he would be able to obtain the necessary documents again. In the meantime, invitations had come to the Lutheran Church in Hungary from a number of countries. So Ordass had no difficulty in arranging a stay of five months abroad, with visits to Switzerland, Sweden, the United States, Norway, Denmark, and Finland. He was unable to visit Austria and Germany since he had only a transit visa but no permit to stay in those countries. He also did not travel to France, because the appropriate people were absent at the time of his travels.

At least seven years had passed since a Hungarian church leader had been able to visit sister churches abroad. Rarely did a church follow the travels of its representative with such great interest.

His departure took place on a Sunday, after he had held the main worship service at the church at Deák-tér; as bishop he was also the pastor of the congregation. Special prayers and a special blessing were said for him before he said good-bye to the church administration and his congregation.

His congregation followed his travels with avid interest. After his return, the meetings at which he reported his travels were held in overcrowded churches and parish halls. At his first presentation in the main church, which seated two thousand, many members of the audience had to stand. Besides his presentation he also submitted an official report to the church administration.

During his vacation at Lake Balaton in the summer after his trip, he happened to attend a continuing education course for pastors that was being held nearby. When the two hundred pastors discovered that he had with him a manuscript of his official report, they asked him to read it to them. When he reached the last part, which contained the financial account, he wanted to abbreviate his presentation because he thought it would hardly be interesting for his listeners and a good deal of time had already passed. But they wanted to hear about this, too. So he had to report how and where he had encountered financial difficulties and how he had somehow always received help. The pastors wanted to hear the most detailed description of the journey that had been followed with such strong interest.

In the course of the five months of his journey, Ordass preached in thirty-six worship services. He gave presentations about his country and his church on forty-four occasions, usually in German, English, or Swedish, a few times even in Hungarian. He took part in clergy convocations and annual church assemblies, spoke at theological institutes and youth conferences, took part in congregational gatherings, and also attended the Lutheran World Conference in Lund. He conducted innumerable negotiations, wrote articles for church papers and magazines, gave interviews, and still found time to visit the sick among the Hungarian immigrants in the United States.

He received generous pledges for further assistance to Lutherans in Hungary, especially from the sister churches in North America. Ordass negotiated for the support of teachers, organists, widows of pastors, deaconesses, and diaspora pastors, as well as for the repair of churches and the purchase of bicycles. Seminarians needed food, and the library of the Theological Faculty and other church libraries needed foreign theological literature, which had not been available for them for eight years. He also negotiated for stipends for young Hungarian pastors to go abroad and attend conferences and courses.

In addition to these kinds of support for the day-to-day life of the Hungarian church, Ordass found support abroad for certain plans for the future. One such plan was the opening of a Lutheran hospital in Budapest. Another plan, cherished for a long time, was the creation of a Christian daily paper to be run jointly by the Lutheran and Reformed churches. Ordass was able to gain support for both plans from potential cooperating partners in the countries he visited. Thus it was not surprising that his reports and presentations about his travels were stamped by a contagious optimism. Ordass's reports opened up potential new dimensions of service to pastors and congregations. The possibility of reaching broader circles with the gospel was there if the ecclesiastical apparatus could become functional once again. Clergy and laity gained new energy and hope from this concrete and sturdy contact with sister churches and with brothers and sisters in the faith abroad.

Ordass did not conceal the fact that there had also been disappointments during the five-month journey and that not all of his requests had been granted. He did not blame unfavorable circumstances or the opposition party. He explained openly which goals he had not achieved, and he presented proposals for how these goals might be reached in the future.

The many personal contacts that he was able to make during his travels became more important to Ordass himself and to his church than all of his negotiations for material assistance. Friends and former colleagues from his earlier stay in Sweden welcomed him now with open arms and helped him to meet many prominent Christian leaders. In the United States he became the friend of Franklin C. Fry, the president of the United Lutheran Church, the largest Lutheran church in the United States; Fry later became the president of the Lutheran World Federation. Fry accompanied Ordass on a circular tour and took him along to a series of "district conventions" in his church as a speaker. Other leading churchmen, such as Abdel Ross Wentz and the president of the Norwegian Evangelical Lutheran Church, J. A. Aasgaard, provided much counsel and help. The church administrations of Denmark, Finland, and Norway were also quite accommodating.

Many of the people he met on his travels followed the fate of Ordass and his church with great attention. This became quite evident in the written and oral expressions of regard that he received and also, not least, in a number of intercessions on his behalf. Many of these people retained a fondness for Hungarian Lutherans for life. Later Ordass wrote a series of biographical sketches, entitled *People on My Way*. These reminiscences have not yet been published. Their publication would be a significant contribution to the postwar literature of the European and American churches.

In the winter of 1942/43, Ordass had lectured on the Norwegian church struggle, at a time when little was known about it in Europe. Now during his travels he was able to come to know the leading figure of that church struggle better. Ordass met Eivind Berggrav for the first time when Ordass spoke at a convocation of clergy during a week-long visit in Oslo, during which he was able to have long conversations with Bishop Berggrav himself. Later they met again at the first assembly of the Lutheran World Federation in Lund. After his return Ordass spoke enthusiastically of his encounters with Berggrav in an interview given to the Hungarian church paper *Lelkipásztor*. When the conflict between the Lutheran Church and the Communist government developed a year later in the direction of a church struggle, Ordass's opponents labeled him a "Hungarian Berggrav." Those who formulated such a reproach obviously had little knowledge about the Norwegian church struggle and could not understand why the role of a "Hungarian Berggrav" would not be desirable. Ordass himself knew quite well that a Hungarian church struggle could have no similarity to the Norwegian one. The conditions in the Lutheran minority church could not be compared with the structures of the Norwegian folk church. The structure of the church as well as its history and folk character were completely different. Ordass himself formulated in *Lelkipásztor* what he had learned from Berggrav:

> The conversations with Berggrav have made a deep impression on me. He is a fascinating Christian personality. This church leader, who is perhaps the greatest in Norway, told me: "My brother, our church struggle was conducted from the very beginning in such a way that we could never be accused, even with great malice, of pursuing political goals. We conducted unflinchingly our struggle for the defense of the church, based on our confessional writings and on Holy Scripture. No one could assert that we engaged in politics. At the same time, the entire nation followed the struggle for the defense of the church with great respect and understanding. If you should be forced into a church struggle, then, my brother," he said to me, "you must not let political points of views interfere."

The five-month journey created deep impressions on Ordass. He had been able to serve as the indefatigable ambassador of his church and his people. The extensive travel schedule took its toll on his energy, but he had rendered a great service to his church. Undoubtedly, the climax of his journey as the representative of a modest minority church at the periphery of Europe was when he was granted an honorary theological doctorate from Muhlenberg College in Allentown, Pennsylvania. The constituting assembly of the Lutheran World Federation was also unforgettable; during the assembly he was elected to the Executive Committee, which made him a vice president. Anders Nygren, who had been his teacher during his time of study in Lund, was elected president, and Abdel Ross Wentz was elected second vice president. The American Sylvester C. Michelfelder, with whom he had become friends during a week-long stay in Geneva, became general secretary. His election together with such leading personalities honored and also challenged him. Unfortunately, he was never able to exercise his office because the situation in Hungary prevented any other journey to sessions of the Executive Committee.

The financial difficulties he faced throughout his travels were hardly a highlight of his trip. Ordass, who had a good sense of humor, told about them only among friends. He had not been blessed with material goods during his journeys as a student, nor now as a bishop. Now and then he was even at the edge of poverty. He was not allowed to take along Hungarian money, so he had to finance the whole journey, including the round-trip airfare to the United States, with loans and honoraria from abroad. In Switzerland he had to have a painful tooth pulled. His last twenty Swiss francs went to the dentist for treatment. If the dentist had charged any more, Ordass would have been unable to pay the bill. Although he was well dressed by Hungarian standards, he felt like a gray sparrow in the West, so he enjoyed it all the more when he could buy a few shirts and socks in Stockholm with an honorarium of fifty crowns for giving a presentation. During an evening stroll with a Hungarian stipendist he got rid of his old mended socks by throwing them solemnly into a public wastepaper basket in the Swedish capital.

Ordass's presentations and sermons exuded the enthusiasm with which he did his entire work during these difficult postwar years. His sermon during the assembly in Lund clearly expressed this enthusiasm. It focused on the saying "While it is day." Not discouragement, but a hopeful vision for the future marked his words:

> It is not evening. Let yourselves be persuaded by God's own word. A new beginning can be granted to humankind by the grace of God. There is the morning of the harvest. Behold, how rich it is! Tell your despairing co-workers. Let us make it known now: God gives us a bright day. Let us repeat again and again: We must labor while it is day.

Undoubtedly, such words proclaimed in 1947 by a voice from Eastern Europe must have made a deep impression.

12. Ecumenical Responsibility

THE YEARS after World War II were very fruitful for the cooperation of the churches throughout the world, especially in Europe. Hungary was no exception in this regard. After long years of isolation, Christians wanted to come to know others, to exchange ideas and experiences, and to strengthen each other in faith and service. The Norwegian bishop Berggrav characterized this mood in the title of a booklet, *The Longing of the Churches*.

Ordass was no dreamer regarding the ecumenical movement. But he did expect much from the contacts of the churches beyond national frontiers, particularly in the spiritual and theological realms.

He saw a great opportunity in the challenge of viewing the common Lutheran confessions as the basis for a community beyond national frontiers. He sought first contacts with Lutheran sister churches and their leading personalities in his travels abroad. Already at the beginning of his journey, as a participant in the consultations of the Committee on Relief and Reconstruction of the World Council of Churches in Switzerland, he was confronted with a problem that affected all ecclesiastical relief organizations: Should interchurch relief be administered by regional organizations in each recipient country or given directly through confessional channels? A majority in the World Council supported regional organization; representatives of the Lutheran churches, especially the American churches, argued for confessional organization.

Ordass agreed with the second position, and not just because of his own theological posture. The Lutheran Church in Hungary had always cherished its own confessional character. The evangelical churches, Reformed and Lutheran, had been a minority in the land since the Counter-Reformation, when the Roman Catholic Church had gained the majority. And the Lutherans were a minority within the minority. Thus there had always been an urgent need to preserve the Lutheran identity. During a brief period in the nineteenth century, Hungary, too, was touched by Protestant drives for unity in the wake of the Prussian union. But the Hungarian Lutherans always stood up for the Lutheran Reformation. Accordingly, the interchurch relief for Hungarian Lutherans was given through the Lutheran World Federation, while the Reformed sister church was supported by the World Council.

Ordass could rely on the full backing of his church when he joined the drive for Lutheran unity that had climaxed at the assembly in Lund. He wanted to make sure that the many delegates from all over the world received an impression of the life of the Lutheran Church in Hungary. He brought with him a seventy-page pamphlet entitled *The Hungarian Lutheran Church of Today*, which had been printed in English in Lund, and to which he had contributed a preface. In addition, three Lutheran stipendists from Hungary, Vilmos Vajta, George Pósfay, and Béla Leskó, then students in Sweden, put together a small exhibition. Both enterprises were much appreciated.

When Ordass was elected vice president of the new World Federation, he felt particularly obligated to commit himself to Lutheran cooperation in Eastern Europe, an idea he mentioned already in his report about his journey. The contact between the small Lutheran diaspora churches was to be strengthened through mutual visits and common conferences. He arranged the first Eastern European Lutheran conference and proposed that it be held at the new center of the Hungarian Lutheran Church that had just been established in Fót, fifteen miles north of Budapest.

Such an idea was then not only revolutionary in Eastern Europe but almost utopian. At the time it was extremely difficult to travel beyond national borders, and there was also the barrier of language. The six to eight Lutheran churches that were to gather represented just as many languages. Moreover, the various peoples of Eastern Europe had unfortunately kept separate for many decades.

The peace treaty after World War I stipulated the dissolution of the Austro-Hungarian monarchy. Czechoslovakia, Rumania, and Yugoslavia had become independent states, and each of these states had received a piece of the former Hungary. Within the borders of each of the three countries there was a significant Hungarian minority: in Czechoslovakia there were over a million Hungarians, in Rumania almost two million, and in Yugoslavia half a million. In the first two countries attempts were made to integrate the Hungarians through harsh minority policies. This may be understood as a reaction to the merciless Hungarianization during the monarchy; such policies were also designed to secure the new borders against territorial claims from the remaining Hungary. Hungary, on the other hand, conducted a systematic revisionist foreign policy in order to regain the lost territories from the neighboring countries.

During World War II, Nazi Germany forced the three neighboring countries to return a portion of the territories to Hungary. But this policy was, of course, repealed after the war, and the borders of 1919 were restored. Each change of borders caused a great deal of bitterness.

The relationship between Czechoslovakia and Hungary became especially tense when the countries concluded an agreement in 1946 regarding resettlement of their minorities. A part of the Slovak population in Hungary was to be exchanged for Hungarian groups of people in Czechoslovakia. Ordass was confronted with this problem in various ways. When the agreement became known in Hungary, frightened Slovaks sought him out because they were afraid of a forced settlement of the small minority of about 200,000 Slovaks, just as the German minority had once been resettled. But their fears were probably groundless because only volunteers were to leave the country. On the other hand, the Czechoslovakian government determined who had to leave the country. The number of emigrants was to equal that of the voluntary emigrants from Hungary, together with other groups. The Lutheran Church felt particularly responsible for the Lutherans among those who were expelled from Czechoslovakia. Most of them arrived in Hungary with only a few suitcases.

Few among the Slovak minority were interested in leaving Hungary. A delegation of the Czechoslovakian government came to Hungary to push for the emigration. Three members of the delegation, Lutheran clergy from Slovakia, sought out Ordass and asked for permission to use Lutheran churches in connection with this action. But Ordass refused. The churches would be available for regular services of Word and sacraments, but not for meetings of a political or propagandistic nature.

This stance lost Ordass some support, even in circles abroad. He felt that some individuals in Switzerland and in the United States saw him as a Hungarian nationalist who was guided more by political than by ecclesiastical interests. The misunderstanding was resolved. But it showed how strained the relations were between the two neighboring countries and between Lutheran Christians on both sides of the border.

Despite this experience, or perhaps because of it, Ordass did not abandon his vision of an Eastern European conference of churches. He had spoken about it with leading personalities in the sister churches in Western Europe, especially during the meeting in Lund. Everybody encouraged him to move forward. He discussed plans at various opportunities, especially with representatives of the Slovak Lutheran Church. They, too, reacted positively. In order to make a modest beginning, the Slovak Lutheran Church invited a pastor from Hungary to attend a clergy convocation in the spring of 1948 in their own country.

The invitation to a conference in Hungary came at the beginning of the same year and was to be extended to the Lutheran churches in Austria, Poland, Czechoslovakia, Rumania, and Yugoslavia. Unfortunately, the plan could not be realized. The Hungarian authorities refused to issue entry permits to possible participants in such a Lutheran regional convocation. Thus the very first initiative had to be postponed. Only eight years later did such a conference for Lutheran minority churches take place, and then it was held in Austria under the direction of the Lutheran World Federation. And Ordass was unable to participate in any way.

His strong commitment to cooperation among Lutheran churches did not at all prevent Ordass from seeking contacts and cooperation beyond confessional boundaries. Reformed and Lutheran pastors had always helped each other in the service to dispersed members of congregations in the diaspora, in pastoral care, in education, and in proclamation. No mixture of confessions had resulted. Both clergy and laity had retained a clear sense of confessional identity.

Already in the midst of the war Ordass had been elected to be one of the two secretaries of the newly founded Ecumenical Council in Hungary. This council was formed when Ordass's fellow student from Uppsala, Dr. Nils Ehrenström, visited Hungary in the spring of 1943. The council had a Reformed and a Lutheran secretary; Ordass was the first to hold the latter position.

Even though ecumenicism was not Ordass's first priority, he had great hopes for the constituting assembly of the World Council of Churches in the summer of 1948. He was to lead the delegation of his church there. In an interview immediately before the assembly, Ordass stressed the importance of interchurch cooperation as it had existed during the hard years of the war. It was existentially important, Ordass said, that Christians from various denominations and various social systems and nations, who lived at least in part in tension with one another, could unite to hear the Word of God and to pray together. He hoped that the assembly in Amsterdam would become "a workshop of the Holy Spirit."

The assembly took place. But Ordass himself was not permitted to travel to Amsterdam.

13. Dark Clouds on the Horizon

At the end of World War II Hungarian society began to experience sweeping changes. One epoch was finished, and a superannuated system of society, marked by feudal and aristocratic structures, had become extinct. It had become clear in broad circles of society that the old system could no longer survive. But neither the politicians nor the ordinary citizens in Hungary knew that the Western powers had made an arrangement with the Soviet Union designating Hungary as part of the Soviet sphere of interest at the end of the war. Only gradually did people become aware of the direction of social changes.

Ordass and many others in the church did not lament the loss of the old system of society. The Hungarian church press had never been afraid to provide a platform for critics of society, publishing essays critical of the government, society, and the prevailing ideology at a time when such criticism was risky.

Ordass's stance during the war years was commonly known. It was not by chance that he was asked in 1945 to chair a committee that was to investigate the political attitudes of Lutheran clergy, teachers, and other employees during the war and the German military occupation. Such committees were formed at universities, vocational organizations, larger offices, and industries. Their findings and conclusions could decide the future of one's vocation. At almost every place of work people were dismissed because of the financial crisis, and whoever did not display a clearly national stance was dismissed first. Ordass refused to participate in the work of such a committee. The church could not agree with the government's demand to investigate the political stance of the workers in the church, Ordass said. These workers must be evaluated on the basis of the church's own criteria, and the church had its own competent organs and court of discipline to perform this task.

The desire for a new order led to sweeping changes of societal structures. Some of the changes had detrimental consequences for the church. This was especially true with regard to comprehensive agricultural reforms, which dispossessed owners of large estates of their land and distributed the land to the former farmhands. This reform also affected church real estate, but this first stage of the agricultural reform did little damage to the Lutheran Church. The situation was quite different a few years later, however, when forced "collectivization" dispossessed the new landholders as well.

Still worse was the judicial system after the war, and not just in the days immediately after the liberation. It often became violent "street justice" without any interference by the police or other authorities. "People's courts" were formed everywhere in the land, sometimes at random and sometimes by cleverly staged assemblies, and their verdicts were regarded as legal. The churches, too, were not safe from the encroachments of these "courts." When Ordass was convinced of the innocence of an accused church worker, he tried to take the case to the very top, even though he was hardly ever successful.

One of the four bishops of the Lutheran Church, Zoltán Túróczy, was sentenced to ten years in prison by a "people's court" in the fall of 1945. The church administration was convinced that Túróczy was innocent. Everything possible was done to secure his release, but many months passed before he was freed.

Túróczy was a well-known evangelist, one of the leading minds of the awakening that had a strong influence in the Lutheran Church of Hungary in the 1930s and 1940s. The awakening had various roots. Already at the end of the nineteenth century, missionaries of the Church of Scotland conducting a mission to the Jews had a strong influence on the Reformed and Lutheran churches in the land. After a visit by Bishop Raffay to Finland in the beginning of the 1920s, contact with Finnish Lutheranism became quite intensive. Hungarian pastors spent time studying in Finland. They learned Finnish and were quite impressed by the lively awakening movements there. Nearly all of the almost five hundred Lutheran congregations in Hungary were influenced by the awakening during this time.

Túróczy was well liked in his city, Nyiregyháza, and had friends in all churches. When he was finally released from prison the bells of all the churches in the city rang for a whole hour regardless of denominational differences.

In the fall of 1945, when the press and radio were operating normally once again, Ordass, the youngest bishop, was asked by the other bishops to coordinate the Lutheran programs in the governmental radio broadcasts. But gradually the government began to assert more control over the program. Ordass was instructed that only sermons whose manuscripts had been examined and approved by censors should be broadcast. Ordass was of the opinion that only the bishop had the authority of oversight of Christian proclamation; censorship from outside the church had nothing to say here. At first his arguments were received with understanding, and the radio administration approved a rule according to which Ordass could select the preachers and examine their sermons in advance. But soon there were new conflicts with the radio administration. When even the choice of a Bible text was criticized, Ordass had to tell the administration that further cooperation would no longer make sense. He would no longer be involved in the production of the Lutheran broadcast. The program, to be sure, still announced "thirty minutes of a Lutheran broadcast," but only music was broadcast. Later, Provost Kemény took over the coordination of the Lutheran broadcasts, and a compromise proposal was accepted by both sides.

In time, more and more key positions in society were filled with people who, though not directly opposed to the church, still showed little understanding or favor for the church. Future difficulties were foreshadowed when the authorities in 1947 no longer acknowledged the Reformation Festival of October 31 as a holiday for Protestant workers. The same happened with regard to Good Friday a year later. Traditionally, these two days were the most significant holidays of the Protestants. On these days churches were usually filled to bursting point. Now the country needed accelerated production, and any absence from work was severely punished. But all that was but an early skirmish of the serious struggle between church and state. The parochial schools became the area of the greatest conflict.

The churches in Hungary had always been exemplary in their care for public education. In the middle 1940s various ecclesiastical communities were responsible for about 70 percent of Hungary's schools. The Lutherans were particularly dedicated to developing their own school system. At that time, the small Lutheran Church maintained four hundred elementary schools, fourteen secondary schools, three teachers' training colleges, and a school of law. Most of the teachers' salaries came from the government, so that the government had control over the curricula used. But the church schools had their own textbooks.

The Lutheran congregations had strong ties to their schools, which were known throughout the country for their high standards. The Lutheran Gymnasium Fasor in Budapest graduated several Nobel Prize winners, and students in the Lutheran schools had always been successful in national championships for higher education. The Lutheran congregations sacrificed much for their schools, and their members commonly sent their children to Lutheran schools even when it might have been financially more advantageous to let them attend the public schools, which in many cases were located right next to parochial schools. After the war, the parochial schools were the first to open, thanks to help from sister churches abroad and the admirable support of parents.

Already at his installation as bishop Ordass had addressed the question of the future of parochial schools, for it was commonly known that the government aspired to a reform of schools. Ordass knew that the authorities had sent a representative to his inauguration. The government assigned this task to the secretary for church and education, Albert Bereczky, who was later a bishop of the Reformed Church. Bereczky mentioned the schools in his speech. He expressly assured the audience that the authorities "had never considered limiting the services of the parochial schools or refusing them governmental support which they could claim." After the last war and in the face of the prevailing poverty in the country, he stated, the government did not even have the necessary means to take over the schools. Bereczky said that there was no intention of taking over the schools without substitutes.

This statement of the state secretary appeased Ordass and other leaders in the church. But already a year later Ordass had to cite crude attacks against parochial schools in his report to the annual meeting of the synod. The government had assured the freedom of the schools, but the press of the Communist Party had sounded the alarm against the parochial schools. In the wake of such attacks the media of other parties, especially of the Socialist Democratic Party, sounded a similar note. Ordass insisted that the Lutheran Church would secure the service of its schools with its own means. The schools were the pride of the church. Their curricula and education had served precisely in the interest of a better future, which everyone desired and for which everyone fought. They had never discriminated against anyone because of lack of money or social status, or because of their background.

During his journey abroad in 1947 Ordass received the news that the government had prepared plans to repeal the obligatory instruction of religion. The minister for church and education, Gyula Ortutay, justified this action with the claim that such obligatory religious instruction was widely unknown in other countries. Already during the journey Ordass had put together documentary evidence that, together with comparable documentation of the Reformed and Roman Catholic Churches, proved the contrary and made it impossible for the government to achieve its intention.

In the course of the year 1947 the political climate worsened noticeably under the growing pressure of the power of Soviet military occupation and of the Communist Party. More and more leading politicians were replaced with Communist Party members. Worst hit in this regard was the party of the small farmers, which had received 57.7 percent of votes in 1946. Even though this party had a clear majority, the Communists took over more and more important government positions. In 1947 they had gained three ministers in government: the deputy prime minister; the minister of justice; and the minister of the interior, who had authority over the police and also over a newly established security police, which developed into the real power in the country.

The security police constantly produced new "evidence" of "conspiracies" that were said to have originated in the party of the small farmers. Ordass kept abreast of these developments in Hungary during his journey. When the parliament refused to cancel the immunity of the general secretary of the party of small farmers, Béla Kovács, he was abruptly arrested by the Soviet military police. Six years were to pass before he was heard from again. Prime Minister Ferenc Nagy from the same party preferred to "bail out" during a visit to Switzerland after he had heard by telephone from Budapest that he, too, had been counted among the "conspirators."

Despite all the dark clouds on the horizon, whether in public life or in the life of the church, Ordass could call the year 1947 a year filled with hope and expectation. The Lutheran Church had gotten on its feet again, not least thanks to help from sister churches abroad, and congregational members exhibited a loyalty like never before. The "awakening" had brought vitality into the lives of congregations. There was hope that the church could find its place in the new society and that its service would be respected.

The year 1948 was to be celebrated as a jubilee year in all of Hungary, for a century had passed since the revolt against Hapsburg. Later the year 1948 was called by the Communists "the year of the great turning point." It would become obvious that this year was also to be a fateful year for the Lutheran Church. And Bishop Lajos Ordass would find himself in the center of the storm.

14. As If a Curtain Had Opened

On march 2, 1948, Ordass flew to Zurich via Prague in order to take a train to Geneva, where a meeting and some conferences had been scheduled. The memory of that day remained indelibly in his mind as long as he lived. As he once put it: "It was as if on that day a curtain opened and I could get a glimpse of my own future."

An older gentleman, János Tessényi, senior of the Methodist Church in Hungary, and his wife were on the same plane. He was very agitated. As soon as the plane reached Swiss air space, he spoke to Ordass, asking for a confidential conversation after they landed in Zurich. Ordass gladly agreed.

Tessényi told him that he had been arrested in broad daylight in Budapest. He had been brought to the headquarters of the security police at Andrássy Street, where the German security police (Gestapo) had once been housed. There he was thoroughly interrogated, focusing on his contacts in the United States. But he was also asked what he knew of Ordass. They allowed him to travel to Switzerland in order to spy on Ordass. He was to report about people Ordass met and if possible also about the content of his meetings. To prove the truth of what he said, he showed Ordass a sheet of paper with a series of questions under the name Ordass for which answers were expected from Tessényi.

Tessényi told him at the end of the conversation that he did not intend to return to Hungary. He hoped to travel to friends in the United States. He left the sheet of questions with Ordass.

From this day on Ordass knew what he had to expect. The meeting and conference in Geneva proceeded as planned. During his stay in

Switzerland he heard the news about the coup d'état in Czechoslovakia, about the death of the foreign minister Masaryk, and about the takeover of the Czech government by the Communists. Before Ordass left Switzerland, he received the news that the Social-Democratic Party of Hungary had been forced to complete its merger with the Communist Party on March 15.

He told a few friends abroad and the three Hungarian stipendists in Sweden about his conversation with Tessényi. The farewell from Michelfelder, the general secretary of the Lutheran World Federation, was moving and cordial. After two weeks abroad Ordass was again in Budapest, and he went about his work as if nothing had happened. Not even his wife or his closest co-workers were informed about the conversation in Zurich. But from this point on he never left his official residence alone. He wanted to have a witness in case he was arrested in broad daylight. Often Irén Ordass accompanied her husband on walks or on official trips, without knowing that it might perhaps be for the last time.

Already in the beginning of 1948 there were signs that the year would be less quiet than the previous one. The pressure of the Communist Party increased everywhere. Although a peace treaty had been signed in 1947, the Russian troops remained in the country. The official explanation for this was that the connection with the Russian occupation troops in Austria had to be secured. But in fact the Russian troops were an obvious and not to be disregarded support of the Communist Party in Hungary. Mátyás Rákosi, the general secretary of the party and also deputy prime minister, gradually became the "strong man" in the country.

The increased political pressure was soon felt in the office of the bishop. Ordass received a series of inquiries and complaints, first from teachers in the service of the church who had been threatened with dismissal if they would not become members of the Communist Party, and soon also from pastors throughout the diocese who reported the same problem. The news media increasingly used a sharper tone regarding the church.

During the first half of 1948 several figures appeared on the political stage with whom Ordass and the Lutheran Church would gradually have quite a lot to do. The journalist Ernő Mihályfi (born 1898) would play a major role in later events. He was the son of a Lutheran pastor but had distanced himself from the church early on. During the war he worked for the underground press. After that he became a politician;

he first represented the party of the small farmers, but soon found his way in the new situation. He was minister of propaganda for some time. In 1948 he worked for the prime minister as his personal secretary of the interior, with the rank of a minister. Later he chaired the Hungarian "Peace Council," became deputy chairman of the Hungarian-Soviet League of Friendship, a member of the board of the "People's Patriotic Front," and editor-in-chief of the paper of the Front, *The Hungarian Nation (Magyar Nemzet)*. Finally, he also became a member of the highest governing body of the country, the Presidential Council.

The author József Darvas (born 1912) had a similar background. He had made a name for himself as a popular author in the 1930s, portraying the problems of the farm proletariat in the form of novels. Already as a student he had embraced a Marxist view of life and had played an active role in the Communist youth movement in Budapest, according to Hungarian and Soviet records. The Hungarian historian of literature Gyula Borbándi, now living in Germany, reports that Darvas had said publicly at a meeting of the Evangelical Academy Loccum in 1967 that he had been a Communist for thirty years. He had not had a trace of interest in the church until he, like Mihályfi, was assigned by the government to take part in the negotiations with the Lutheran Church.

The surgeon Ivan Reök had quite a different career. He had been for some years an active member and worker in the Lutheran Church. He experienced a conversion in the 1930s and appeared quite often as an evangelist and presenter, together with Bishop Túróczy. His book *A Surgeon Encounters God* appeared in several editions; some of his evangelistic presentations also appeared in book form. Beginning in 1947 he had dedicated himself mainly to politics, especially as a member of the parliament.

No one could guess in the beginning of 1948 that these three men, each in his own way, would play a decisive role in the history of the Lutheran Church of Hungary and would be instrumental in accommodating the church to the Communist government.

Ordass had learned upon his return from Switzerland that Ernő Mihályfi was to give a presentation the next day at the clergy convocation in Budapest. A politically active pastor and teacher of religion, László Gaudy, had invited Mihályfi to participate. This presentation by Mihályfi was the first of a whole series of similar activities in which he consistently represented the viewpoint of the political rulers vis-à-vis the Lutheran Church.

His presentation turned out to be a frontal assault upon the church leadership. He demanded that the lay leaders in the church administration, that is, the "inspectors," should withdraw, and thus the church structure should be renewed along the lines dictated by the political rulers.

The office of the "inspectors" in the Hungarian church cannot be compared with similar offices in other churches. According to a centuries-old tradition, "inspectors" were chosen in a special election. They were expected not only to provide administrative, indeed spiritual, leadership but also to take on the task of protecting the church from attacks and abuse of power from the outside, whether from the powerful Roman Catholic Church or from the power of the state. The general inspector shared the office of president of the National Council of the Lutheran Church with the highest ranking bishop. He had his own office, managed by the general secretary of the church. The other governing bodies also always had a double presidency: a pastor and a layman shared responsibilities. Accordingly, the inspectors exerted significant influence on all levels of the church. Most of them exhibited great loyalty and a touching fidelity. The national hero Lajos Kossuth, for example, who had to flee the country after the battle for freedom was lost in 1848/49, remained an inspector of his home congregation until his death in exile in Italy forty-five years later; he remained in contact with his congregation by correspondence.

Mihályfi now demanded that the inspectors should be elected according to political norms. With a threatening voice he warned the church "not to offer shelter to reactionary forces behind its walls"; and he attacked certain church leaders by name. No one could complain about the situation in Hungary, he said, except those who were enemies of the people. He rebuked the church because it had done nothing so far "to regulate its relationship with the state."

Ordass was not present on this occasion. But already the next day he heard the same charges and accusations when Mihályfi repeated them at the installation of the new Lutheran bishop in the city of Balassagyarmat. The bishop of the district "on this side of the Danube" had resigned for reasons of health. His successor was József Szabó. On this occasion Mihályfi represented President Tildy, who had been invited but could not come. Mihályfi presented his critique not in the church but at a special meeting to which he called the entire church leadership after the service of installation.

The chairman of the college of bishops, Bishop Béla Kapi, who led the district "on the other side of the Danube," responded to Mihályfi in a controlled manner and with reconciling words. The church had not taken the initiative to negotiate with the government, he said, because they had the impression that such an initiative was not desired. But now they knew about it and would make an effort to make contact. Ordass was equally controlled in his manner, but he rebuffed the accusations of Mihályfi point by point. There was no exchange of views. But from now on the church leaders and Mihályfi, the mouthpiece of the party, knew their respective positions. At this time Ivan Reök also became active in church politics. Reök let it be known that he was close to the leader of the party, Mátyás Rákosi. In any event, he gave Ordass and other church leaders the impression that he knew quite well what kind of opinion the authorities — that is, the Communist Party — held of the Lutheran Church.

Finally, church leaders had no choice but to go directly to the most powerful man in Hungary, Mátyás Rákosi, in order to ascertain his attitude to the church. On April 19, Ordass had an audience with Rákosi, accompanied by the new bishop Szabó and the lay inspector of his own diocese, Gábor Vladár. The two-hour audience contributed much to clarifying the situation. The conversation disclosed that Reök had appeared before Rákosi as the authorized representative of his church. He had made incriminating but false statements to Rákosi about persons in the church, including, among others, the general inspector of the church, Albert Radvánszky, and the chairman of the college of bishops, Béla Kapi. Despite these disturbing disclosures, it was enlightening to know from the highest authority what the confidant of Moscow demanded from the Lutheran Church.

The Lutheran Church was expected to acknowledge and support unequivocally the social revolution of 1947/48. Further, the church was to change its leadership, which represented a "remainder from a bygone time." The church should agree to have its schools taken over by the state. There should no longer be obligatory instruction of religion. In addition, the diaconical work of the church would be superfluous in a socialist society, since such tasks would without exception be done by the state.

Ordass immediately requested a meeting with Reök after the encounter with Rákosi. They talked by themselves. Ordass confronted Reök with the false accusations that he had spread among his own friends in the church and had passed on to Rákosi. Ordass had checked the charges out and found that they were not true. It was not true that Radvánszky had assisted the Fascist Szálasi in his introduction as chief of state. It was also not true that Bishop Kapi had signed a letter beginning "Hail Szálasi." Ordass further stressed that a series of Reök's statements regarding ecclesiastical governing bodies were unfounded and damaging to the church. Reök had arbitrarily told the National Organization of Women, dominated by the Communist Party, that the organization of women in the Lutheran Church had joined that Communist organization, but this was not so. He had also printed his own political program on the program of a church concert, and so on. Reök made excuses and tried to defend himself by pointing to his baptism through the Holy Spirit, contending that Ordass had proven himself in speech and action as one who was not so baptized.

Further events developed with increasing speed. Conferences took place, each one followed by media attacks. The demands of the government — that is, those of the Communist Party — were formulated with increasing clarity. Ordass forced himself every night with admirable self-discipline to write down the most significant conversations and events of the day, despite his great fatigue after a strenuous day of work. It is a miracle that these notes were not found when the house was searched later in the summer. With the help of these notes, it will be possible for a church historian to reconstruct many details of what happened in the year 1948, but that contribution to Hungarian church history is still to be written.

As events unfolded with increasing speed and attacks on the church grew in intensity, it would soon become evident that Ordass had indeed seen his future through the "curtain" that had opened.

15. A Matter of Identity and Integrity

IT BECAME clear to Ordass during his negotiations in the spring and fall of 1948 that the church could not accept the demands of the state without losing its own identity and integrity as a Christian church. To be sure, the top leadership of the church had declared a kind of loyalty to the state in connection with the centennial of the 1848 revolution. But the church could not go so far as to throw off its leadership under pressure from the outside to substitute officials who would show sympathy to "the new age."

Among the most faithful pillars of the church, many of whom were in positions of church leadership, were men who had held high public offices before the war. For example, a former minister of justice became the inspector of a church district in the fall of 1947. Changes in Hungary had brought great changes in the lives of many church members. People who had once been rich now lived in poverty and misery after their possessions had been confiscated. Former landowners had to go to the homes of agricultural laborers as boarders in order to survive. Ordass told Mihályfi that the church did not have to follow the example of the state. People who had been loyal to the church had now been marginalized in society. The church had not closed its doors to those who sought consolation and help during the war. Mihályfi should remember, Ordass stressed, that the Lutheran churches at that time were filled with people who wore the Jewish star of David. Could the church now, after the social revolution, exclude people from its ranks who were marginalized? In reply, Mihályfi countered that it was the task of responsible church leaders to nurture trust in government, and the church should not steer into a bloody cultural battle.

Regarding schools, Ordass recalled that at his installation as bishop State Secretary Bereczky had given assurances that the state did not intend to take over the parochial schools. As late as April 1948, the authorities had negotiated curricular matters with the parochial schools. So why was Mihályfi suddenly talking of the necessity to nationalize the same schools? Moreover, promises had been made to negotiate about schools "in a quiet atmosphere"; but now more pressure was felt than peace.

Little resulted from these conversations.

In April 1948 Béla Kapi resigned as the head of bishops. Bishop Túróczy was able to take the office of bishop again in the meantime, even though he had not yet been acquitted. That is why he did not want to accept the office of head of bishops. So Ordass had to step in and became for a brief time the mouthpiece of the church in the negotiations with the state. Meanwhile Mihályfi and Reök lobbied for the full rehabilitation of Túróczy and were successful after a few months. They thought they might find him easier to work with in negotiations.

At the end of May the government submitted a draft of a document concerning church relations, "An Agreement with the Lutheran Church." A series of paragraphs dealt with the service of the church and its relationship to the state. The church was to entrust the schools voluntarily to the government. In return, the government would guarantee obligatory religious instruction in the schools and would give the church financial support to pay the salaries of pastors and other expenses. This support would be reduced in stages and would cease after twenty years. Following a decade-long tradition, the bishops explained the situation to the congregations in a pastoral letter that was also printed in the Lutheran church paper *Harangszó*:

> For centuries our congregations have supported our schools with dedication and kept them alive with an infinite willingness to sacrifice. Today our congregations still love the schools. This is witnessed by the anxiety with which our friends follow the destiny of the schools. There are many reasons for such anxiety, which is shared by the church leadership. Until recently, we had assurances that the schools would be able to continue their service. The plan to nationalize the

schools appeared quite unexpectedly. It was especially upsetting to see our teachers put under pressure to propel this nationalization on their own. Thus these co-workers of our church have come into conflict with their respective congregations and also with their own oath of office. It is further upsetting that at evenings with parents open voting in favor of nationalization is arranged — and with parents who showed their loyalty to the parochial schools by the fact that they send their children to these schools and sacrifice much for them. It is also sad that the media one-sidedly condemn the parochial schools and find no good word for their indisputable services and their excellent standards.

Then followed a description of the negotiations about the "Agreement" submitted by the government, and the assurance that the church leadership would not take any decisive steps in the matter until the appropriate organs of the church had offered their reactions. The congregations were asked to consider well their own reactions to this important matter.

We ask the congregations to formulate their reaction with prayer and invocation of the Holy Spirit, knowing that the expressed desire to keep the schools can mean a stronger financial burden for the congregations because of the lack of support from the state.

The letter closed with the wish and prayer that God might grant foresight and wisdom to the church people and their leaders to make the right decision for the future in this critical situation.

The pastoral letter was signed by the three bishops, Ordass, Túróczy, and Szabó, and also by Károly Németh, the vicar bishop who substituted for Bishop Kapi. But it became evident that not all bishops shared Ordass's view of the critical importance of the schools. The new bishop Szabó and above all Bishop Túróczy tended to regard the question of schools as a secondary matter that did not touch the vital interests of the church. They were inclined to accept the "Agreement" because of the promise of obligatory religious instruction and the financial support of the government.

During the first negotiations about the "Agreement," a member of the government delegation, the minister for reconstruction, József Darvas, took the offensive against Ordass and the Lutheran Church. He owed gratitude to the Lutheran Church, he said, since he himself had attended a Lutheran school. But now times had changed, and the church had to adjust to the demands of a new era. The church should relinquish its schools in order to assure a united education throughout the country. He was disturbed by Ordass's position and had to conclude that the Lutheran Church was on the path toward a reactionary stance that could not be tolerated in the new society.

Under pressure from many sides, Ordass explored the sentiment in the church. In the beginning of June he attended assemblies in various locations in his church district. He reported about the negotiations and presented the alternatives the church had to face. One possibility was to keep the schools and the democratically elected church leadership, thus perhaps losing the financial support of the government. But he did not want to hide the other alternative, namely, subjecting to the demands of the state, which would result in the "voluntary" relinquishing of the schools and the dissolution of the entire leadership of the church — and perhaps the retention of the financial support of the government.

In the course of these assemblies Ordass met with pastors who served about half the Lutheran Christians in the land. He asked the participants for clear expressions of opinions concerning the "Agreement." With the exception of one pastor, these pastors supported the position of the bishop, who was willing to negotiate but not to give away all the schools. The pastors of small diaspora congregations, which survived only through the modest support of the government, were also among the supporters of Ordass's position; they risked their livelihood through their stance.

At this time, the "Movement of Friends," a revival movement within the Lutheran Church that had been shaped by pietism, held its annual assembly of several hundred members in Fót near Budapest. Bishops Túróczy and Szabó attended. Ordass could not attend because of important official business. The participants used the occasion to assure the two bishops that they fully supported Ordass's position. A common intercession for Ordass constituted a dramatic conclusion of the assembly. Ordass could now be certain that the congregations were with and behind him.

New negotiations took place, which involved the Church and Education Minister Gyula Ortutay as well as Mátyás Rákosi. Their demands were clear: the church must provide new leadership and must sign the "Agreement" about voluntarily relinquishing the schools. The church delegation was summoned to a meeting with the head of state, Tildy, at his villa at Lake Balaton. Darvas and Mihályfi were present. They read aloud segments of sermons that Ordass had delivered during the recent weeks when he had visited congregations. He could not doubt that this material was intended to incriminate him.

A few days after this meeting, the Hungarian parliament formally resolved to nationalize all private schools in Hungary — that is, decided to take them over without restitution. This decision of June 15 was unanimous; after the elections in May, the parliament consisted only of Communists and their vassals.

Already a month earlier the church and education ministry had launched a vehement attack in mass meetings against private schools, calling them "hiding places of the reactionaries." The party media and their hangers-on had understood the signals from on high and attacked the churches and schools without restraint. The focus of the attacks was Ordass. The newspaper *Light (Világosság)* published a bold headline on June 6: "Where does Ordass hide his American dollars that he collected in the U.S.A.?" Any response to such attacks or attempt to show their falsehood was out of the question.

Ordass was to lead the delegation of his church to the Assembly of the World Council of Churches in Amsterdam, beginning August 22. He knew that he would hardly receive a passport. One week before his scheduled departure Mihályfi told him that he could not travel. But anyone who was nominated by the Lutheran Church except for Ordass would receive a passport to travel. When the Lutheran Church showed itself in solidarity with Ordass and did not nominate any other delegate, the government was indignant and alarmed. The church authorized its three stipendists in Sweden and a layman who was in Paris to represent the church in Amsterdam. Ordass had been scheduled to lead one of the morning prayers at the Assembly. The young stipendist Vilmos Vajta took on this task. Ordass's absence caused a great stir. The news of his arrest became known in Amsterdam only two days after the opening of the assembly, which lasted for two weeks. Telegraphic inquiries brought forth contradictory responses. The telegram of Prime Minister Lajos Dinnyés assured: "He is neither under house arrest nor in any other way detained. He is completely free and does all his religious functions." Another telegram explained that the arrest of Ordass concerned monetary business, not church service.

No one in Amsterdam believed that Ordass had violated currency regulations. Representatives from churches of all continents declared their solidarity with Ordass. The bishop of South India, who presided at the concluding worship service, named Ordass in the intercessionary prayer of the congregation. Ordass was elected to the Central Committee of the World Council.

The three Hungarian stipendists had to return to Sweden. Two of them, György Pósfay and Béla Leskó, had already begun their journey home to Hungary when the General Secretary of the Lutheran World Federation, Sylvester Michelfelder, who knew the latest developments, asked them not to return home and to serve world Lutheranism and thus their own church abroad. Pósfay was for many years pastor of the multilingual Lutheran congregation in Caracas, the capital of Venezuela, until he became Secretary for Latin America at the Lutheran World Federation in Geneva in 1971. Leskó became a parish pastor in Buenos Aires and later director of the theological academy there. Vilmos Vajta had been asked earlier by Ordass to remain in Sweden in order to expand contacts between Lutherans in Hungary and the Swedish church. Four years later, Vajta was called to be the director of the Department of Theology of the Lutheran World Federation; he later became director of the newly established Ecumenical Institute of the Lutheran World Federation in Strasbourg.

What had really happened in Budapest? Ordass had indeed been arrested on August 24, together with General Inspector Radvánszky and the general secretary of the church, Sándor Vargha. At the same time, Ordass's home was carefully searched. Numerous books, personal papers, and the bound diaries were taken and never returned. The search of Ordass's home lasted three to four hours, until the policemen finally became tired. One desk drawer remained untouched. It contained the most recent diary entries and a series of other confidential notes.

Ordass was kept waiting for almost a whole day in an empty hall. Now and then a police officer entered and opened a drawer at a desk to get a few pistols. He played with them, inspected their loading, and returned them to the drawer. Ordass was finally taken to interrogation at 4:30 in the afternoon. At issue was the money the church had received from abroad. In the evening he was led back to the same hall. He had been given neither food nor drink and had to try to get some sleep on chairs he had pushed together. Soon he was awakened and taken home. He was told that he was under house arrest. But the arrest was suspended the next day. It was clear that the first telegram from abroad had reached the authorities, asking for an explanation of Ordass's arrest.

One week later the Lutheran Church was told that Ordass had been given a deadline of September 8, at noon, to give up his office as bishop.

Meanwhile, Mihályfi asked the church to tell the Lutheran World Federation by telegram that Ordass was free and could exercise his office without any interference. Since Ordass's only alternatives were prison or resignation, they refused to send a telegram about it — a risky business, given the ruling terror in the land.

The authorities then made a second attempt to get rid of Ordass. He was told through Bishop Túróczy that he and his family could volunteer to leave the country. Ordass immediately replied that he had no intention of doing so.

Three days before the deadline, on Sunday, September 5, Ordass led the worship service in the main church at Deák-tér and preached on the text for the day, the introduction to the story of the resurrection of Lazarus (John 11:1-11).

> Let us understand correctly the message of this Sunday. Jesus wants to imprint in our hearts with letters of fire the teaching that we cannot avoid: The love of God and the tests he sends us do not exclude each other.

The concluding sentences would become the last words he was to speak from the pulpit for eight years.

> Before we say farewell to each other let us hear something that can inflame our hearts. Our text says, "But Jesus loved Martha and her sister and Lazarus" [so in the Hungarian translation]. Let us add our own names here. I wish I could go from one pew to the next, call each one of you by name, and say, "Jesus loves you." After he has now consoled and strengthened all our hearts, let us then step to the side of the apostle of love and love him just as John did. For he loved us first.

The critical situation was particularly troubling to Ordass, for he knew that the Reformed Church had given way to the pressure and had signed the agreement demanded by the government. This fact had been used to pressure the Lutheran Church even more. Even more troubling was the fact that the constant pressure had now also begun to demand sacrifices in the ranks of his own church.

A large number of Lutheran pastors from the whole country were called by Mihályfi to an assembly in Budapest on September 7. Ordass himself had not been invited, and he was not surprised by that. What surprised him was that the three other bishops and a large number of pastors accepted the invitation, even though Mihályfi had no authority to summon ecclesiastical officials. Those who were present heard Mihályfi's sharp attacks against Ordass without opposing him. Finally, they accepted Mihályfi's proposal to single out a group of three pastors who would immediately advocate "the true concerns of the church": Vilmos Gyöngyösi, Károly Gyimesi, and László Dezséry. Dezséry had confirmed at an earlier time in a conversation with Ordass that he had not left the ranks of the Socialist Democratic Party when it was fused with the Communist Party, and thus he was a member of what was called the "Party of the Laborers." He was to play a key role in the dramatic events that concerned the Lutheran Church during the fall of 1948.

The deadline for Ordass's decision to resign or to be arrested came at noon on September 8. In the morning of the same day, church leaders assembled one more time for consultation and prayer. At noon, Bishop Túróczy called the minister of the interior to tell him that Ordass had no intention of resigning.

Ordass went home to wait for the arrival of the police. They came only after sundown.

16. A Mock Trial

THIS TIME he ended up in the cellar of the same building where he had been interrogated two weeks earlier. The cell was damp and narrow. For three days he was left alone.

Then, together with Radvánszky and Vargha, he was taken to a prison where a record was established. The public prosecutor told him, with almost exaggerated courtesy, that he was being imprisoned until his trial. His companion in the cell was an honest, warm-hearted peasant farmer from Jászberény, defendant number 103 from a large "conspiracy" that had been "exposed." The cell was roomy, but dirty and run down, with unpleasant surprises. Hordes of lice attacked the inhabitants at night. The bishop reported later that he commenced a counterattack and was able to count 134 dead lice at dawn.

The next day he was transferred to a larger cell. There were six plank beds, which had to be shared by thirteen prisoners. The prisoners came from all corners of the country and from various social levels, and they had been arrested for various "crimes." A young director of a factory had been promised release if he would volunteer to resign from his position. He signed the statement of resignation, but instead of being released he was laughed at and returned to the cell. An artist had been arrested because he happened to be in a train compartment with someone who wanted to leave the country without permission. A young man of about twenty years had been caught stealing potatoes. He was the oldest of nine siblings. When Ordass asked him why he had wanted to steal, he responded, "Because we had nothing to eat at home."

As soon as the prison doors closed behind Ordass, the media began to spread wild rumors about him and about his two "accomplices." "They have embezzled tens of thousands. They have damaged the Hungarian state by hundreds of thousands: Bishop Lajos Ordass, Albert Radvánszky, and Sándor Vargha. They abuse their high offices in the Lutheran Church." So proclaimed the newspaper of the Communist Party, *Free People (Szabad Nép)*, two days after the arrests. A headline covered the whole front page of the newspaper *Light (Világosság)*: "The list of transgressions of the arrested Bishop Ordass, Albert Radvánszky, and Sándor Vargha." They were not accused of small crimes. The newspaper *Hungarian Day (Magyar Nap)* summed up the matter with the headline: "To what end did Ordass and his gang use the money of the church?" And below it read:

> Widows of pastors received fifty forint, but they themselves bought villas. It became evident that the money, which was designated for the work of the church and for charity, was embezzled in the headquarters of the church and was used for private purposes. Six million forint had been spent in the course of recent years, without any control, by Ordass, Radvánszky, and Vargha. Even a minute inspection could not ascertain where the money went.

The same article reported that the Lutheran Church had received 800,000 forint from the government for reconstruction, but only 300,000 forint had been used for this purpose, while half a million ended up in a private bank account. "Their crimes are unparalleled."

The prisoners finally saw some newspaper articles. Ordass had been prepared for something even worse; during the interrogations he had also been accused of raping minors. Such accusations could hardly have damaged his reputation, however, for the Hungarian people had gradually learned to see through such unrestrained slander.

He received handcuffs and shackles for the first time when he was given an opportunity to inspect his dossier. The exact reading of the indictment became a pleasant surprise. As far as he was concerned, the indictment was significantly milder than one would have guessed, given the agitation of the media. He had "deliberately neglected" to report the gifts of dollars from abroad to the National Bank, so it read. Moreover, he had "taken out a loan" in 1947 in Sweden in order to finance his journey to the United States. He had always been open about these financial matters, for to him it was most important to have a completely pure conscience. The Swedish loan was expressly mentioned in his report about the journey, which enumerated all his income, expenses, loans, and so on. He had even described all these details at clergy convocations when he reported about his journeys.

The public prosecutor dropped this part of the indictment. It was really the general inspector of the church who was responsible for any formalities regarding help from abroad. The authorities had always been informed about these transactions, and they had been executed without exception by the National Bank. Ordass had also talked with the director of the bank a few days before the arrest in order to make sure that everything had been done according to valid rules and mandates. The director could assure, without hesitation, that there had been no irregularities. The whole matter would not even have come to a trial had there been a "normal," neutral court. But "the issue here is something quite different than the control over some monetary transactions," as the director had put it.

Ordass had no doubt that it was not a matter of formal points of indictment but of finding an excuse to remove him from the leadership of the church. The entire nature of the indictment, which focused on "economic crimes," suggested that a severe verdict was to be expected. In addition, his case was tried not before a regular court but before a "people's court," also popularly known as a "usury court." It was commonly known that these courts issued particularly strict verdicts, for the government wanted to punish severely all those who damaged the economy of the country or the new currency, the forint.

Ordass remembered well a visit to his old congregation Cegléd shortly after the forint had been introduced in 1946. At the same time, a high government official, István Kossa, had visited the town. He warned of harsh punishment for all those who misappropriated the new currency. One sentence of his speech became the headline in the local newspaper: "We will hang people, indeed we will." The same Kossa later became the director of the office for church affairs, which the Communists instituted in 1951. His threats against economic criminals were still fresh in people's minds when Ordass was arrested.

When Ordass was finally able to speak with his defense attorney, he received clear advice. He had to be prepared for anything, "from two years to the death sentence." The defense attorney, Dr. János Kardos, was known to be an honest man who did his best. Ordass had not known him personally before, but he knew that Kardos had just been elected

A MOCK TRIAL

inspector of a district of the Reformed Church. Kardos told Ordass that he had also been nominated as a candidate for a national inspector position, but he had declined because he could not hope for good cooperation with Albert Bereczky, the new bishop of the Reformed Church.

Ordass concentrated on Bible reading and prayer, as far as it was possible to collect his thoughts in a crowded cell. He was allowed to have his Bible. The trial was to take place within three weeks. The possibility of a death sentence could not be excluded. But God blessed him with inner peace and tranquility. He decided not to appeal for mercy in case of a death sentence.

Dr. Kardos's defense was later called a masterpiece. He succeeded in refuting the indictment and the arguments of the public prosecutor piece by piece with inarguable logic. The president of the people's court, who had to prove that Ordass had "consciously neglected to report the foreign holdings of the church in a prescribed form," cut such a pathetic figure that Ordass almost pitied him. Eyewitnesses report that the members of the court listened to the reading of the verdict without looking up and then immediately left the hall. They knew that they had taken part in the condemnation of an innocent person.

Ordass was allowed to speak before the court withdrew to decide the verdict. Several listeners recorded his speech word for word. These were the voluntary stenographers in his church, who normally recorded each sermon preached in the church, for it could be useful to have a precise record in case a preacher was called to account, and the sermons could also be duplicated and sold for the benefit of church renovation. These voluntary stenographers recorded the final words of their bishop before the verdict was read.

> Honored Presiding Judge, Honoured Special Court! I need not add much to what my defense attorney said regarding my case. That is why I want to claim your attention only for a brief time. The proceedings against me have now lasted five weeks. During this time I have had plenty of time to try myself and to ask myself: Did I violate any law? Did I neglect something? Does my conscience accuse me regarding any detail? I have repeated these questions of self-examination also before God in prayer. The answer I received from God was an infinite tranquility of the soul, a tranquility that has carried me without interruption for these five weeks.

Until now I have experienced in my life many blessings and many fruits of my Christian faith, from my days as a barefooted child in a poor teacher's large family in the country to this day when I hold the highest office in my church. Among those fruits is one that is called tranquility. Never before in my life has God granted me such a tranquility of the soul than in these last five weeks, even though these weeks seem suited in every respect to destroy my inner tranquility. I have done my service publicly. I am convinced that I have done it in the interest of society and for its good. When I returned from my journey abroad, a journey that has been often mentioned in the trial, I requested in my official written report that the church leadership should not express any gratitude, either in public or in personal conversations, for the service I was permitted to do with good success under the blessing of God.

It is quite self-evident that I do not expect any gratitude from my homeland. I had never thought that this matter should be worth mentioning. Had I ever thought about the matter, it would have been at the utmost as a modest contribution to the reconstruction of my devastated homeland and my church. I repeat: my service was a public service. It is known that anyone who fights for something in a public position can also be wounded. I do not want to hide the fact, Honoured Special Court, that I feel the wounds that have been inflicted on me.

You now will withdraw in order to decide the verdict. It is your task to weigh and to examine everything that has been said about me according to your conscience. I do not know what kind of verdict will be returned. If your conscience compels you to an acquittal, then the wounds I carry away from my battle for society will not be so bloody and painful, so that I will be able to do my work with complete dedication and the same fervor as before. It is my intention to continue my service. God will help me to forget these five weeks. I am prepared to continue my service for my homeland and for my church.

It is also possible that you will find me guilty after your consideration and impose a punishment on me. In that case I will accept it peacefully and with humility in my heart. If I am convicted, then the conviction will become a veil that hides God's will from me and renders it incomprehensible to me. But I will accept it from the hand of God without grumbling. One thing I know — namely, that whatever happens to me is God's beneficial will.

A MOCK TRIAL 85

The verdict was returned late in the evening of October 1: two years in a penitentiary, loss of office for five years, loss of all civil rights for the same period of time, and a fine of 3,000 forint.

17. The Cell of the Priests

The main prison in Budapest was ready to burst. Ordass was taken there four days after the verdict, exactly on the twenty-fourth anniversary of his ordination. There was a bulletin board with a variety of information. Old numbers were crossed out, and new ones added. One could figure out that the unit was intended to hold 98 prisoners, but that it now housed 346. The floor space of Ordass's cell was sufficient for exactly four mattresses of straw, which had to be shared by five prisoners. After a few days, Ordass's Bible was taken. It was never returned.

He remained in the main prison for one and a half months, and then he was transferred to the "Star Prison" at Szeged near the Yugoslavian border. This was an enormous structure in the form of a star, known and feared throughout the whole country. A particularly strict unit was reserved for political prisoners.

Ordass spent three weeks in a single cell "under observation," after which he was taken to a larger room, where he lived together with fifteen Roman Catholic priests. This group remained together without any change for fifteen months.

As a rule, Hungarian church history of the last 450 years is depicted as an unceasing battle between Protestants and Catholics. Not only spiritual weapons were used in this battle. Protestants were often persecuted and oppressed at times when the house of Hapsburg ruled its Catholic inheritance with a hard hand. Protestant textbooks consciously kept alive the memory of the persecutions. The result was a division between the two communions so complete that any reconciliation or

THE CELL OF THE PRIESTS 87

dialogue was out of the question. The authorities used this chilly atmosphere whenever they could to play one communion off against the other. For this reason the life in "the cell of the priests" was truly remarkable: a Lutheran bishop was able to share a cell for fifteen months with Catholic priests without any incident of hurtful remarks or outbreaks of impatience. The nerves of the prisoners must have been frequently so tense as to burst, but the good spirit of comradery was maintained. Ordass contributed to this good atmosphere already at his arrival. He gave a brief speech before his fellow prisoners. Their confessional differences should not prevent them from living together like siblings, he said, for they had in common Jesus and his gospel. They had all been in his service, and their will to remain loyal to him had delivered them to this common fate. His cellmates agreed, and life together in the cell developed not only into a good human relationship but into a true Christian community.

Their assigned work was to spin flax. No one felt humiliated by such work, for there was an advantage in being able to spend their time usefully. But it was unjust that the clergy had to do their work in their cell, while the other prisoners had a special shop. Each morning the straw mattresses had to be piled on top of each other in order to make room for the spinning wheels and other tools. Even more burdensome was the air in the cell, which became so dusty that one person could hardly see another when the floor was swept in the evening; afterwards they had to sleep in this room.

Ordass had been accustomed from childhood to do practical work. Soon he was classified as an "excellent worker." This meant that he earned twenty-eight forint a month, while others earned only seven to twenty forint. Workers had to pay one forint for one loaf of bread. They even received a voucher for white bread at the "fir festival" on December 15. But Ordass did not cash it in.

In the beginning, prison conditions were relatively liberal. The prisoners were allowed to receive packages weighing up to ten pounds. Whoever had money could even subscribe to a newspaper. Prisoners were allowed to read literature for entertainment and even theological books. Every two weeks the prisoners were allowed to participate in a worship service, priests every Sunday. Two times per day they were permitted to walk a round in the inner yard. Once a month they could receive visitors — that is, a close relative could have a conversation of ten minutes with the prisoner in the presence of a guard. Once a month they were given permission to "shop" in the prison kiosk, where there was bread, fruit, and canned goods.

After some time, a number of restrictions were put in place. The weight limit for packages was reduced to four pounds, and one could borrow only ideological books from the prison library. The clergy soon became totally familiar with such literature. When the light was turned off in the evening, lively discussion took place about what had been read.

Later the four-pound packages were allowed only every other week, and every sort of reading and writing was prohibited: books, newspapers, writing paper, pencils, and pens. The Catholic priests were robbed of their breviaries, which they used for their meditative life. Ordass had been deprived of his Bible already in the main prison in Budapest.

In the final phase, all packages and visits were prohibited. They all had to wear prison dress. Even the work was ended.

In the beginning they had been allowed to write and to receive one letter a month. But Mrs. Ordass and her husband had agreed not to correspond because of censorship. At first Mrs. Ordass was able to visit, but later she had to be hospitalized again so that she could no longer visit. The link to the outside world was now completely cut.

Ordass, of course, knew nothing about the sympathy and attention caused abroad by his arrest. He also knew nothing of the attempts to prove his innocence. A great cloud of intercessions surrounded him. When Bishop Gustaf Aulén conducted a worship service on Swedish radio at Christmas 1948, he mentioned his former student Ordass in the intercessionary prayer. Ordass's name was mentioned all over the world when there were prayers for persecuted brothers in the faith.

The prisoners heard news of the outside world only through the guards, who did their work mostly without any noteworthy enthusiasm for the political system that was responsible for the overcrowding of the prison. But this way of receiving news was very unreliable. Rumors were here in full swing, as in other East European countries. It was difficult to distinguish between reliable information, propaganda, and sheer wishful thinking.

But it was possible to form certain conclusions about developments in the country in other ways. The arrival of new prisoners in the prison indicated the new targets of the "people's democracy." For a while "kulaks" or independent farmers who had resisted the collectivizing of

THE CELL OF THE PRIESTS

their farms arrived. Later, only goldsmiths or millers arrived, so it was clear that the government was busy collectivizing these enterprises. At another time, the victims of certain mass trials ended up in the Star Prison. One could also tell when voluntary government "bonds for peace" were imposed. Many who did not sign for these bonds experienced the same fate as those who refused to "volunteer" to turn over their farms and businesses to the state.

At one time, the prisoners became indirect witnesses of the execution of five "kulaks," four men and one woman, who were accused of murdering a village secretary of the Communist Party. A special court sentenced all five to death; the sentence was executed in the Star Prison. The prisoners knew of such events because they were awakened later on the day of the execution and their morning round in the yard was cancelled. Two weeks after the execution one of Ordass's cellmates came into possession of a newspaper in which they could read that the killer of the party secretary had now been found and arrested.

According to the usual rule, a prisoner could be released for good conduct after having served three-fourths of the sentence. Ordass could have applied for his release in the beginning of March 1950. But he did not do so, for he knew that prisoners who made the application had to undergo a thorough ideological testing before the director of the prison. The director tried to extort a confession from them, saying that they regretted their attitude and were willing to become loyal servants of the people's democracy. Ordass did not want to expose himself to such a test. One of the Roman Catholic priests had applied for release from the final quarter and so had come into a very uncomfortable situation.

Church news rarely or never filtered through to the cell. The newspapers early on had more to report about the results of production and successes of the system of the people's democracy than about the church and Christianity. News about the church consisted mainly of ever more violent attacks against the Roman Catholic Church and its primate, Cardinal Mindszenty, who was finally arrested on the day after Christmas in 1948. Shortly before Christmas, Ordass discovered the only news he was to receive about the Lutheran Church in a note in *The Small Paper (Kis Ujság)*. It noted that the Lutheran Church had signed an agreement, a concordat, with the Hungarian government.

Ordass recalled his final visits in his congregations and his conversations with the pastors and the church leadership. They were clear witnesses of unity in difficult times. The signed "agreement" could only mean one thing: the church had handed over the schools to the government and had received a new leadership.

He could not fathom it. What had happened?

18. The "New Era" in the Church

It was clear to the authorities from the beginning that Ordass was not alone in his stance. The church leadership had supported several of Ordass's statements in the spring of 1948. The pastors were behind Ordass, both at the level of senior districts and at the national level. An assembly in the middle of June, with participation from the whole country, was a clear proof of it. Representatives of the awakening movement had expressed themselves in a similar way. Congregational assemblies also made it clear that Lutheran Church members believed they should keep the parochial schools and bear the resulting financial burdens.

All this was not unknown to the authorities. Often it became clear during the negotiations that they were informed about the atmosphere in the Lutheran Church. Ordass was told more than once that he was responsible for the "unrest" in the church since he "pressured" teachers and other employees of the church to resist the authorities. The minister for church and education, Ortutay, once made a remark about "a Mister Keken" who involved himself in the question of parochial schools. Ordass had responded that this "Mister" was the pastor of the main church in Budapest, who, after a congregational assembly, sent a report to the ministry that the largest Lutheran congregation was also unwilling to separate itself from its schools.

The authorities had hoped that fear would spread in the church after the arrest of Ordass. But they soon had to recognize that this would not be brought about with the removal of only one person. Moreover, their goal was to create the impression that the whole church had decided in favor of the "Agreement."

A first strategic move was to grant the church advantages on which it could count only after signing the "Agreement." To these advantages belonged, among other things, the continued financial support of the churches, guarantees for theological education at one of the universities, and obligatory religious instruction in the nationalized schools. In a second move, they used threats and demonstrations of power to show those who were uncertain that further resistance made no sense and that the authorities had the power to execute their plans in any case.

The general secretary of the central church administration, Pastor Sándor Vargha, was the first leader to be arrested. The arrest took place on June 10, 1948, when Ordass was still involved in negotiations with the representatives of the state. Ordass let it be known that further negotiations would be conducted only after the release of Vargha. He was released the next day.

After Ordass had been arrested for the first time in August, Vargha was also again apprehended. At the same time, the general inspector of the church, Albert Radvánszky, was also put into custody. All three were arraigned together. But Radvánszky was a little older and was a heart patient, and he had to be taken to a hospital shortly after his arrest. The charges against him were dropped from the trial and later stayed. Vargha was tried with Ordass and was sentenced to three years in a penitentiary. But before all this happened, both Radvánszky and Vargha had "volunteered" in prison to resign from their offices.

Two other leading Lutheran pastors were arrested during the preparation for Ordass's trial. One was Pastor András Keken, the other was György Kendeh, Ordass's successor in the congregation of Kelenföld. Both were extensively interrogated in connection with the indictment of Ordass, and the security police issued continuous reports about their "confessions." Together with Ordass they had prepared a conspiracy led by Ordass, the reports alleged; another report claimed that they were engaged in espionage. At least Ordass was not indicted on these charges. Keken and Kendeh were no longer interrogated after his conviction. Conspiracy and espionage were no longer mentioned. Both pastors were taken to a work camp without any trial.

Another strategic move was the spread of doubt, confusion, and feud in the church. The newspapers were completely controlled by the rulers, so that the church press had to exercise a great deal of constraint in its statements. It did not take much for the church press to lose its allotment of paper.

It was easy for Mihályfi to provide an effective and broad publicity for the stance of the government. At the end of August he gave a speech that was printed with bold headlines on the front page of the largest daily newspapers. The demands of the state were bluntly set forth, with attacks against Ordass. Church leaders "who do not support without reservation our new democratic society and love this system" must resign immediately. Persons with democratic convictions, who sympathized with the people and the new reforms, must be elected in their place. Concrete proposals were made in this connection. Among others, the surgeon Ivan Reök and the writer József Darvas were mentioned. Moreover, Mihályfi demanded that "a democratic church assembly" should be called in order to make "an agreement with the state about the schools" and, in general, "create new forms for the life of the church in the system of the people's democracy and create the presuppositions for a common effort toward the reconstruction of the country."

The convention of pastors that Mihályfi summoned on his own on September 7 received broad publicity; one newspaper even proclaimed it as "the assembly of the democratic church leadership," even though it was a private gathering. The board of three that had been elected by this convention — the pastors Gyöngyösi, Gyimesi, and Dezséry — visited a number of leading churchmen and demanded that they resign. The whole matter had become so public, and the danger of arrest so threatening, that quite a few obeyed the demand. Thus three of the four inspectors of church districts resigned. Bishop Kapi resigned because of old age, and Vargha and Radvánszky had signed their farewell petitions in jail.

In the fall no one had precise information about events. The church paper *Új Harangszó* had been prohibited shortly after Ordass's arrest. Immediately afterward, the campus pastor Dezséry published an "Open Letter about the Lutheran Church" to the pastors, which had a large distribution. The thirty-page letter attacked the church leadership and repeated the same charges that Mihályfi and other representatives of the rulers had enumerated before, both in speeches and in other ways, above all before the captive press.

It was unthinkable that paper would have been allotted to a church official in order to respond to Dezséry's "Open Letter" in public. But Dezséry himself was permitted by the authorities to edit a weekly journal entitled *Lutheran Life (Evangélikus Élet)*. When the paper *Új Harangszó* was again allowed to appear after six weeks, there was no news in it about the arrest of Ordass and other church leaders. The "Open Letter" of Dezséry was mentioned, however, along with the news that Dezséry was now one of the editors of *Új Harangszó*.

The confusion among the pastors and in the congregations grew more and more, and it was intensified when the new journal of the campus pastor Dezséry printed an address allegedly given by Bishop Túróczy. This address promoted a stance clearly different from that of Ordass, although Ordass was not actually mentioned. Yet only half a year earlier Ordass still had the broad support of his entire church!

The address declared that if someone issued a warning in this situation and called for caution, then that person was engaging in "political speculation." Church leaders certainly must not risk the life of congregations "and those who trusted them through meaningless dramatic heroism" and "without a command from God." What the church now needed, the address declared, was not "rumor mongers who hide in the dark, not boasting Goliaths, not clever and sly diplomats, or political dreamers." What the church needed now was rather "people who had the courage to seek God's will in obedient struggle and to bear witness openly and responsibly about their visions."

After all the stops were pulled out in this manner, the Lutheran Church finally submitted to the demands of the rulers. A synod, the legislative organ of the church, was convened to adopt the agreement that the authorities had submitted already in May. The synod clearly showed that the church had been deprived of its proper leadership. Only one of four bishop's offices was filled. Lay leadership consisted mostly of substitutes. This was the kind of church assembly that sanctioned the agreement with the government under constant threats.

Many who voted for the acceptance of the concordat secretly hoped thereby to gain the release of Bishop Ordass. But such hope soon evaporated. On the contrary, the government now demanded that the church elect a new bishop, thus relieving Ordass from his office once and for all.

The anxiety and confusion increased in the whole country, and also in the Lutheran Church, when Cardinal Mindszenty was arrested at the end of 1948. If the government did not shrink from prosecuting the spiritual leader of the powerful Catholic Church, then anything was possible. The regime of terror of the "Rákosi era" materialized, and gradually no one dared anymore to express an opinion in public that contradicted the rules of speech of the rulers.

Ordass knew nothing in the Star Prison in Szeged about this new situation in the Lutheran Church. But he got an impression of these developments in the beginning of 1949 when he was called to the office of the director of the prison. He was to have a conversation there with two visitors from Budapest, Bishop Túróczy and a pastor from his own diocese.

Túróczy first brought greetings from Mrs. Ordass, who was under medical treatment in a Budapest hospital. But his real purpose was to inform Ordass about his case. The authorities had pressured the church to take Ordass's case also to an ecclesiastical court. But Túróczy himself had stated that no disciplinary court of the Lutheran Church would condemn Ordass. He had also raised the question with Rákosi whether Ordass might be allowed to leave the country. Rákosi, however, no longer showed any interest in such a solution. But if Ordass would volunteer to withdraw from his office, he would be pardoned and granted a state pension. If he would not provoke the government, he could eventually be pastor of a congregation. Túróczy also mentioned that the situation of the church had changed during the last six months. Even Mrs. Ordass had said that she would soon be able to count the supporters of her husband on the fingers of one hand.

Ordass maintained that he could not accept the pardon, but only a just acquittal. It was his opinion that a bishop may not resign under the threat of political authorities. But if he truly no longer had the confidence of the congregations, he would volunteer to resign. But it was impossible to ascertain the true opinion of the people in the church, given the existing circumstances.

Túróczy and his companion arranged with the director of the prison that they would leave to have lunch and would return later in order to receive Ordass's final answer. In the meantime the director allowed Ordass to take a Bible to a cell and be alone for an hour and a half.

He spent the time in prayer and Bible reading. First he looked up biblical passages that dealt with the relationship between Christians and temporal authority. Again and again he read Romans 13, as well as Acts 5, with their well-known sayings about obedience to God and to human authority. He consciously searched for reports about witness to Christ in situations similar to his own. Finally, he arrived at Acts 16, which tells of Paul and Silas in prison. The judge had ordered their release, but they demanded that he should personally lead them out of jail.

The answer he gave to Túróczy was No.

When he returned to his cellmates he discovered that the fifteen Catholic priests had spent the time in common intercession. They knew only that a bishop and a pastor had called on Ordass, and they surmised that there might be a decisive conversation. Thus they prayed to God for him that he would keep his conscience clean. On this day the sixteen prisoners in the cell of the priests became even closer to one other.

A few months later there was another attempt to force him into a "voluntary" resignation. This time it was the new church leadership that asked him to resign. The pastors who transmitted the message quoted "friends in Switzerland" as urging his resignation. Ivan Reök, now the general inspector, had visited Switzerland, together with Bishop Szabó. Now they brought greetings from "friends in Switzerland." This could only have been a reference to the leadership of the Lutheran World Federation, of which Ordass was vice president. He received the greeting with the greatest distrust. Later it became known that it was fabricated.

Ordass's answer this time, too, was No. But the political authorities did not let the matter rest with his refusal.

Top: Main street in Torzsa, where Lajos Ordass spent his childhood. *Right:* Lutheran elementary school (and the teacher's residence, where he was born). *Left:* Lutheran parsonage.

Above: The school building (photo from 1983)

Left: Altar of the Lutheran church in Torzsa. The church was raised in 1810, torn down at the end of the 1940s.

Elisabeth University, Lutheran Theological Faculty (1922-1951), Sopron, Western Hungary

Main Lutheran church at Deák Square in Budapest. Ordass was ordained here to the ministry in 1924, to the service of a bishop in 1945.

Left: Lutheran church in Cegléd, with monument of the national hero Lajos Kossuth
Right: Altar in the church in Cegléd

Religious instruction in the diaspora ("dispersal"), 1930s

A new church bell arrives for the Lutheran church in Cegléd. The pastor speaks from the back of the lorry.

Lutheran church in Kelenföld, Budapest. *In the center:* congregation hall (with sliding wall to the church). *Both wings:* housing for the church staff.

Lutheran church in Obuda, Budapest, before World War II

The Obuda Lutheran Church after World War II

Left: Ordass with Lutheran World Federation General Secretary
S. C. Michelfelder, Geneva, Switzerland, 1947.
Right: Bishop Zoltán Túróczy (photo from 1957)

Clippings from the Hungarian Communist press reporting the
"crimes" of Lajos Ordass, September 1948

> Blessed be the God and Father of our Lord Jesus Christ, the Father of mercies and God of all comfort. He comforts us in all our affliction so that we may be able to comfort those who are in any kind of affliction by the comfort which we ourselves are comforted by God. For as we have more than our share of suffering for Christ, so also through Christ we have more than our share of comfort. But if we endure affliction, it is for your comfort and salvation; and if we receive comfort, it is for your comfort — the feeling you acquire when patiently you endure the same sufferings as we also endure. And our hope for you is firm; for we know that as you are sharers in the sufferings, so you are also sharers in the comfort.
> II. Corinthians 1:3-7.

First sign of life from Ordass to reach the West after his arrest in 1948: 2 Corinthians 1:3-7 (1951)

Üdülő Hotel Galyatető, Hungary, site of the international church convention in 1956

Left: Ordass in the pulpit for the first time in eight years (October 14, 1956)
Right: Ordass celebrating Holy Communion at Budahegyvidék Church, on the same occasion

Ordass's appeal to sisters and brothers in faith abroad, November 2, 1956 (in a temporary studio at the Parliament building)

Delivery of aid at the Hungarian border, spring 1957. Shown with Ordass is the Hungarian-speaking Secretary for minority churches in the Lutheran World Federation, Mogens Zeuthen (Denmark).

Funeral for Bishop Béla Kapi (1957). Bishops Kuthy and Ordass in the center. Bishop Szabó is the second on Ordass's left. Bishop Túróczy, performing the funeral, is not in the picture.

Salzerbad, Austria, spring 1957. From the left, first row: Károly Karner, Lajos Ordass; *second row:* Gyula Nagy, Imre Veöreös, Dezső Wiczián, József Szabó; *third row:* Károly Hafenscher, Jenő Sólyom, András Keken.

Salzerbad, 1957. A short time of rest in the garden.

New York, August 1957. In the office of Paul Empie.

Minneapolis, 1957. Ordass met at the airport by General Secretary
Lund-Quist *(center)* and the mayor of Minneapolis, P. Kenneth Peterson.

Minneapolis, 1957. Central Hall. Opening service for the
Lutheran World Assembly, at which Ordass gave the sermon.

Minneapolis, 1957. The new Executive Committee of the Lutheran World Federation. Ordass is second from the left in the third row. Others shown include Bishops Lilje and Smemo *(last row)* and Church President Fredrik A. Schiotz *(center, second row).*

Left: Visiting the grave of Norwegian mission pastor Gisle Johnson (1969). *Right:* Lutheran church in Nagybörzsöny, a remote place north of Budapest, where Ordass's son-in-law was parish pastor for twenty-five years.

Ordass receives visitors from Norway. *From the left:* the author, Mrs. Ordass, Ordass, the author's son Lars, and Bjørn Helge Sandvei (1974).

Ordass at his writing desk, 1975

Ordass with his wife, Irén (1975)

Ordass's funeral, August 19, 1978

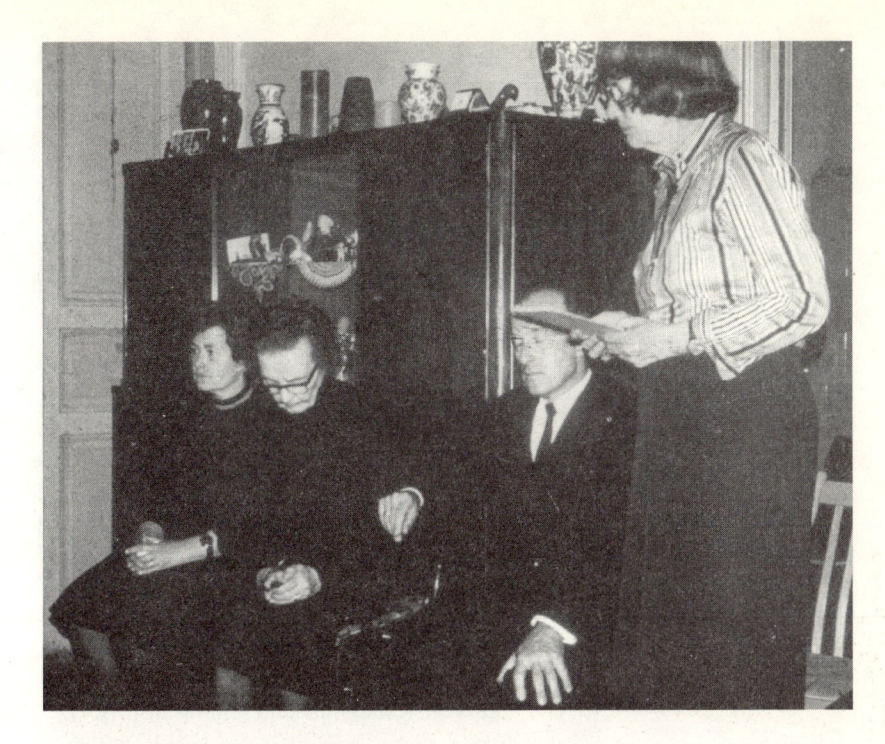

In the Ordass home after the funeral. Mrs. Ordass is in the center. Mrs. Bodil Sølling conveys the greetings of the Lutheran World Federation.

Ordass's grave in Farkasréti cemetery

Interior of Vinje Lutheran Church, Wilmar, Minnesota. The frieze around the wall, "A Cloud of Witnesses," contains names of witnesses from the Old and New Testaments and church history.

Left: Bonhoeffer, Berggrav, Ordass — the last three names in the frieze "A Cloud of Witnesses."
Right: Portrait of Ordass in a Lutheran parish hall in Buenos Aires, drawn by the Hungarian artist Lászlo Dobosi Szabó and unveiled by the dean of the cathedral, later bishop, Ragnar Askmark (Sweden) in 1959.

19. In Solitary Confinement

In the beginning of 1950, rumors spread through the prison that there were plans to transfer the political prisoners to a different facility. According to the newspaper reports, the large prison in Vác at the bend of the Danube was to be taken over by the security police.

On March 15, a Hungarian national holiday, also known as "the day of freedom" in commemoration of the revolution of 1848, the inhabitants of the cell of priests were divided into two groups of eight; each group was linked together and put in a railroad car. The car was coupled to a passenger train and, guarded by armed police, traveled via Budapest to Vác.

A totally different prison life awaited him there. Ordass was put into a single cell, where he remained for the rest of the two and a half months of his imprisonment. Was this a "punishment" for his refusal to resign? He thought it unlikely, but he could not find out whether his fifteen former cellmates were also in solitary confinement, or whether this prison consisted only of single cells. Here he could not keep any personal property. Every pair of socks and even his last handkerchief were taken from him. The cell was austerely furnished. There was a single woolen blanket as protection against the cold spring nights. Here he endured the greatest physical suffering of the whole time of his imprisonment, for a pane was missing from the window and the cold was severe. Every week replacement of the window pane appeared on the list of needed repairs, but nothing was done about it. To make it worse, the prison clothes were suited only for summer. However, the food was somewhat better and more plentiful than at Szeged.

The strict treatment was especially depressing. Insults had not been unknown at Szeged, but the vulgar language of the security police in Vác was unimaginable.

For the first three days he completed the daily walks in the prison yard together with the other prisoners. They had to walk three steps apart in single file, with their hands at their backs and their heads down. The guards often forced them to run. So terrorized, the prisoners complied in order to avoid worse reprisals. Ordass also obeyed the orders on the first two days. But on the third day he refused to run. After the guard had yelled at him to comply like the rest, he kicked Ordass in the shin when he disobeyed. Ordass retorted that he was in the yard to walk, not to run. The guard sent him back to the cell with severe threats. On the next two days, Ordass refused to go out to the yard to "walk." He expected that the result of his disobedience would be what the prisoners feared most: the infamous "disciplinary" or "dark cell." He was surprised when an official in civilian clothes entered the cell and asked politely for an explanation of his behavior. The discussion resulted in permission for Ordass to walk alone and without strict supervision for ten to fifteen minutes in the prison yard each day.

The guard who had kicked him soon used the opportunity of one of these solitary walks to ask, "Why do you treat me so arrogantly?" Ordass replied that the guard was responsible for the "treatment" he was getting and that his manner of treating Ordass was brutal. The guard again drowned Ordass in vulgar insults. But after that day he remained silent. Probably he had been reprimanded by a superior.

Ordass knew quite well that a long period in solitary confinement would entail a heavy psychological burden, especially in light of the fact that his two-year prison sentence could easily be extended. In order to keep his sanity he would have to create a daily regimen to follow. He had no Bible or anything printed at all, and he also had nothing to write with. His only writing implement was a nail. He used it to write stenographic symbols on the door of the cell, describing a strict daily schedule. He intended to follow this order to the letter.

The day began with a morning meditation in English. First he tried to reconstruct a chapter from one of the Gospels. He began with the Gospel of Matthew. After he had recalled as much as possible from the selected chapter (and he was often surprised at how much he was able to remember), he recited the text in English in an undertone. Then he added a free prayer, followed by the Lord's Prayer. A formula of blessing, whichever one he recalled, ended the meditation in English.

The next component of the program he called "A Word for the Road." He imagined that he had to write a book of brief, suggestive meditations on a saying from the Gospels, one saying for each day. He labored to make these meditations fit to print. In fact, he wrote such a book of meditations after his release. It appeared in Hungarian in what was then West Germany. Another series of meditations was published in English in the United States. Both books originated in these prison meditations.

"People on My Way" was also planned as a manuscript for a future book. Here he tried to depict a number of people who had been significant influences on him on the road of discipleship for his development as a Christian. He tried very hard to draw these portraits so well that he would be able to write them down at his desk immediately after his release. The subjects included the parish pastor of his childhood as well as Bishop Raffay and Archbishop Söderblom. The woman who lived next door to his family in Torzsa was also included; when he had left home in order to attend school in Verbász, she had given him a biblical saying "for the road."

In another component of his regimen, which he called "Treasury of Hymns of the Church," he tried to recite stanzas of hymns from memory. He gratefully remembered people who had forced him as a child to learn hymns by heart, and also some who encouraged him as an adult to memorize hymns, as did Professor Deák in Budapest and Sopron.

Another daily component focused on stenography. He had learned stenography in the gymnasium, and he had often used this script to make notes during negotiations. Now he used part of the day to reconstruct the most important stenographic symbols without pencil and paper. He also invented new stenographic abbreviations for widely used words in theology and in the work of the church.

The afternoon program began with an hour of telling jokes. He had always cherished funny stories, not least from the life of the church. Now he intended to organize them according to categories. For example, there were jokes about specific people; Professor Kovács in Sopron was the source of innumerable anecdotes, and many other jokes owed their origin to a certain senior in Aszód. The jokes were organized according to themes: jokes about pastors, hunters, fishermen, aristocrats, and so on. Sometimes he laughed so heartily that the guards burst into the cell, thinking that he had become insane. But it was not really that bad.

The next component of the program he called "The Visitation." Every day he took up a congregation of his diocese. He knew all of them so well that he could picture the whole event: his arrival, the welcoming address of the inspector, his own response, his sermon topic at the worship service, his words to the association of women, to the youth group, and so on. He imagined visits in the diaspora and brief stays with members of congregations who were no longer very active in the life of the congregation. He imagined giving advice at visitation assemblies about the renovation of the organ and repair of the roof of the parsonage. If the congregation of the day was a weak congregation, he imagined ways of making contacts for them with livelier congregations.

The next component focused on literature. Earlier in his life he had translated some works of fiction from Scandinavian languages. Now he planned to treat a current topic in this form on his own. He wanted to depict in a larger novel the history and life of a village under changing conditions. He did write a short novel after his release, which appeared in English in the United States. He also drew up an outline for an autobiography.

Next came the musical part of his day. He knew many folksongs, both the music and the lyrics. Now he organized his stock of songs according to themes. One day he would hum songs about birds, other days songs about stars and seasons, flowers, musical instruments, shepherds or thiefs, and so on.

At the end of the day he did his evening devotion in Swedish. He repeated the same chapter of the Gospel with which he had dealt in the morning. Frequently he recalled additional material from the chapter during the day. Now he translated everything into Swedish, adding a free prayer and some liturgical prayers that he had learned by heart in Sweden. He concluded the Swedish evening meditation with some Swedish hymns, among them an evening hymn that he repeated every evening, and the Aaronite blessing. But at the very end, he prayed in his own language for his neighbors, his family and friends, his co-workers and fellow prisoners, and the church and its ministry.

On certain days he really had to hurry in order to finish everything he had planned to do. He often became so absorbed with some components that time passed unnoticed.

The two and a half months Ordass spent in solitary confinement could have been a dark time in his life. Instead, they became a great blessing for him. But a hard test still awaited him before his time of imprisonment was behind him.

20. A Disciplinary Matter

On April 17 a guard opened the door of the cell and led Ordass to the office of the prison director. There he was given a document to read.

The document had been issued by the disciplinary court of the Lutheran Church and noted that this court had "dealt with the disciplinary matter against Bishop Lajos Ordass" on April 1. It said that the verdict of the "people's court" against Ordass had damaged the interests of the church, and so the church council removed Ordass from his office.

Ordass did not want to believe his eyes. Only one year earlier Bishop Túróczy had told him of a conversation with party leader Mátyás Rákosi in which Rákosi had been told that no court of the Lutheran Church would ever condemn Ordass. Now it had happened after all.

The rationale for the verdict read as follows:

> The special court that judges disciplinary matters sees no reason to speak about the case since that has already been decided by the people's court. However, the court notes that, because of his conviction, Lajos Ordass cannot fulfill the duties incumbent upon him according to church law, and, according to the view of the court, he will not be able to do so in the foreseeable future. This is detrimental to the interests of the church, so the court sees itself compelled to pass the above-mentioned resolution.

The communication was signed by Reök, the general inspector of the church, who was also the president of the court, by the prosecutor Emil Margócsy, and by the secretary of the court, Gyula Groó.

Ordass's original trial and sentence to two years in prison in October of 1948 had been condemned far beyond the borders of Hungary, and now this judgment was equally sensational. The matter could not be discussed in Hungary, whether in the church media or anywhere else. *Evangélikus Élet* mentioned the judgment in a note of five lines. But sister churches abroad immediately asked for clarification. The Lutheran World Federation demanded an explanation of the condemnation of its vice president and published the few records that were commonly accessible. Besides the verdict itself, there was only a twisted statement of the church leadership, assuring that the court had been legitimately called into session and that the judgment had been passed according to church law. More could not seep out of Hungary. In the *News Bulletin* of the Lutheran World Federation, General Secretary Michelfelder added a bitter commentary to the report of the event.

The world abroad knew little; but Ordass himself knew even less in his single cell in Vác.

The year 1948 had been the year in which the Communists seized power in Hungary. But the following year was not less significant; during this year the authorities' aim was to secure the system of the "people's democracy." Just as in other East European countries, so in Hungary the authorities were not choosy about the means used during this "Stalinist" period. In the beginning of 1949, Cardinal Mindszenty was sentenced to imprisonment for life. A series of other trials followed, including the trial of the Catholic archbishop József Grösz. The greatest sensation was the execution in September 1949 of a leading Communist accused of spying, a former minister of the interior and later secretary of state, László Rajk. After the dispossession of the church came the collectivizing of agricultural land. Even peasant farmers, who had received only a small piece of land during the land reform, had to join collectives. Almost every person lived with the threat of being arrested at some point by the security police. One trial after another was initiated and concluded with hair-raising verdicts. The country was in a situation of ever-increasing terror. Even Communist historians today have difficulty finding positive words to describe this period.

In the meantime, some of the leaders of the Lutheran Church did not hesitate to cultivate open contacts with top government officials. Ivan Reök was now the general inspector of the Lutheran Church. In the beginning of 1950, the writer József Darvas took over the same office in Ordass's diocese. The report about his installation in the church paper

Új Harangszó divulged that he was totally unfamiliar with the order of Holy Comunion, which was part of the installation service. It was also the first and last time that he was seen at the communion table. Shortly after he had taken over this ecclesiastical office, he became a member of the Hungarian government as minister for church and education. The issue of *Új Harangszó* just mentioned was one of the last before the authorities withdrew its publishing license.

At the same time, the diocese on the river Theiss had received a new bishop. The former bishop Zoltán Túróczy had changed over to Transdanubia. A majority of congregations wanted to have the parish pastor István Rőzse as his successor. But Rőzse had to withdraw his candidacy under the pressure of the political authorities in order to facilitate the election of their own candidate, Vető. Vető was parish pastor in Miskolc, a large industrial center. When the Soviet troops captured the city in 1944, Vető, who had a good command of Russian and other Slavic languages, had become an interpreter for the occupation power but simultaneously kept his pastoral office. Only 150 people attended his installation as bishop in the large church in Nyíregyháza, where 2,000 worshipers could be counted on ordinary Sundays.

Although the congregations made their attitude known in this and other ways, the new machinery of the church was in full swing.

The general secretary, Iván Reök, was the person principally involved in the events concerning Lajos Ordass. When the government demanded in the beginning of 1950 that the church should begin disciplinary procedures against Ordass, he immediately added another item to the agenda of the next General Assembly of the church: the election of the members of a special court. According to church law a court that accused a bishop should be composed of the general inspector of the church, the three other bishops and their respective inspectors, and six other elected members.

Reök proposed candidates for the six additional positions on the special court, but he was outvoted by the General Assembly, which elected six other persons. But the members of the General Assembly were not satisfed with that. Twenty-seven of them protested in writing against the procedure, indicating that prevailing church law had been violated. Reök found this action outrageous; he was not accustomed to such things in political life. He summoned the leaders of the protesting groups to his office, one by one, and threatened them with reprisals if the document was not withdrawn. Those who did not yield were suspended from their offices. Among them were the seniors Gyula Dedinszky, Pál Zászkaliczky, György Murányi, and Gusztáv Bártfay-Kelló. Dedinszky had an important function in the church leadership. Zászkaliczky was a preacher and evangelist known throughout the country, and the other two also enjoyed high esteem in the church.

But that was not the end of the matter. Three days before the court was to assemble Senior Keken was again arrested, as was Pastor Kendeh the next day. Both had been released from a work camp in 1949 and allowed to exercise their offices again. Now they were accused of conspiracy and espionage. Both were known to be close co-workers of Ordass. Reök made sure that the news of their arrest was quickly spread in the church. They were not indicted but simply taken again to a camp until they were forced to resign from their offices six months later. Finally, Senior Zászkaliczky, who was one of the six persons elected by the General Assembly to be a member of the court, was also removed before the special court assembled. His substitute was the later Professor Károly Próhle. The name of Zászkaliczky does not appear in the report of the church leadership to the Lutheran World Federation.

A few years later a document appeared that threw new light on these events. A member of the special court had left an envelope behind that was to be opened only after his death. He had recorded a series of details on eight single-spaced typed pages regarding the events that had occurred before and after the trial.

Reök had, of course, not succeeded in getting his own candidates elected as members of the special court. It looked as if Bishop Túróczy was still right: no court of the Lutheran Church would ever condemn Ordass. So Reök was forced to use methods of terror. On the day before the trial, the document's author was summoned to a meeting with Reök. The circumstances indicate that every single member of the court was subjected to the same treatment.

Reök stressed in the conversation that party leader Mátyás Rákosi had set a period of two weeks within which the church could settle "the Ordass matter." If Ordass was not deposed before the end of this appointed time, a new trial against him would be initiated, this time with the charges of espionage and conspiracy. The verdict that was to be expected could be for fifteen years or even the death penalty. Pastors Keken and Kendeh, who had already been arrested, would also be charged with the same crimes. Reök said that it had taken all his efforts to prevent the arrest of all twenty-seven signators of the protest. He also knew with certainty that at least eight other Lutheran pastors would be arrested and charged with the same crime as Ordass if the church did not make the decisions the authorities desired.

This was the atmosphere in which the special court assembled on April 1, 1950. The document offers a shocking picture of the desperate position of the members of the court. Eight among them gathered before the proceedings for mutual consultation and prayer, but they could not come to a consensus about what their attitude should be. The document clearly shows the confusion, fear, and anxiety regarding the future of the church that dominated the majority of the members. But it also shows that some followed the party line of the government without reservation, especially Reök himself and Emil Margócsy. Bishop Túróczy and some others tried to call attention to procedural mistakes but could not make themselves heard.

The verdict was attained by secret ballot. Eight members abstained, four agreed with the proposal to remove Ordass from office. When the verdict was declared void six years later, no less than thirteen illegalities had been ascertained. But in the spring of 1950 neither the church in Hungary nor the sister churches abroad, not to mention the "deposed" bishop himself in his lonely cell, could know anything about that.

Ordass felt deeply humiliated when the prison official told him with obvious contempt, after reading the verdict, that now he should no longer complain. His own church had deposed him, so there was no reason to maintain any longer that the government had sentenced an innocent man.

Ordass's entire trust in people had collapsed. In this desperate and humiliating situation he could only cling to his faith. God alone preserved him from sinking into deepest despair, as he repeatedly attested later.

The final eighth of his sentence was commuted. Nevertheless, on May 30, 1950, he stepped with a heavy heart through the prison gate.

21. Only a Spectator

It appeared to Ordass as if he was in a strange land and in a strange church when he was reunited with his family after twenty-one months in prison.

Hungary was about to become a "people's democracy" modeled after Soviet Russia. On August 20, 1949, the Day of Saint Stephen — a national holiday that bears the name of the Hungarian national saint and had been celebrated with fairs throughout the entire country in better times — a new constitution was proclaimed; the significance of the day was emphasized by organized mass demonstrations.

Russian had become the primary foreign language in the schools. Economically, the country was incorporated into the Eastern European structure of the Council for Mutual Economic Aid (Comecon). Even the smallest cobbler shop was taken over by the state, and in the course of a few years 95 percent of the agricultural soil had been nationalized. As usual, Soviet troops were stationed on Hungarian soil. After the conclusion of the Austrian state treaty in 1955, the Warsaw Pact justified their presence. The cult of personality became more and more grotesque. Everywhere one could see pictures of the great Stalin and the almost equally great Rákosi. Virtually every single person was registered in the files of the security police. All publications were censured; even the mail was subject to censorship. It is hard to imagine how a poor country could afford such an apparatus of control. Even the most loyal Communists lived with constant insecurity. János Kádár, the fifth in the hierarchy of the party, was arrested and cruelly tortured. Indeed, the chief of the security police, General Gábor Péter, was sentenced to long and severe imprisonment in 1952.

There was a totally new situation in the church. After the special court of the church had deposed Ordass, proceedings for the appointment of the new bishop were begun. At the customary assembly of the seniors before the election of the bishop, József Darvas, the inspector of the diocese, who was also minister for church and education, declared the candidate Lajos Kemény as ineligible. The only suitable candidate, according to Darvas, was the author of the "Open Letter," László Dezséry. After the publication of his letter, Dezséry had been forced on a Budapest congregation as their pastor, despite their protests. The party apparatus went to work once again, just as it had done at the election of Bishop Vető in 1948: local party secretaries "happened" to call on the parish pastors to inquire how the congregation intended to vote. Dezséry was, of course, elected and was installed to the office of bishop in the summer of 1950. A few years later, Dezséry divulged to a guest from Sweden with a certain pride that party leader Rákosi had read his "Open Letter" and had called him the suitable successor of Lajos Ordass.

The synod was summoned again in 1952, in its capacity as the legislative organ of the church, to issue church laws that would better correspond to the new era. It was a dramatic assembly. In the course of the session the general inspector, Iván Reök, was forced to resign. Obviously, he had not been sufficiently successful. Immediately thereafter, Ernő Mihályfi was nominated as the only candidate and elected to this highest lay office in the church. The same man who had begun the agitation of the coordinated media against the Lutheran Church four years earlier, and who had effected the most significant changes of personnel in the church behind the scenes, was now to have the highest honorary office in the church.

The age limit for pastors in the Lutheran Church was reduced to sixty, thus getting rid of a whole generation of pastors who were distant from the development of the "people's democracy." Since most of the seniors were also older than sixty, almost the entire leading stratum of the church was exchanged. Under the pretext of streamlining the administration, the four dioceses were merged into two: a northern and a southern district. The bishops Túróczy and Szabó were forced to resign, and Dezséry and Vető took over their church districts. The congregations were not consulted.

What hurt Ordass most was the fate of his friends and co-workers Keken and Kendeh. In the fall of 1950, they had been released a second time from the labor camp after they had written their letters of resignation. After that they made a bare, uncertain living as casual laborers in the capital. In 1951, "unproductive elements," among whom Keken and Kendeh were classified, had been deported from Budapest on a grand scale in order to create living space for the workers of the expanding industry.

Keken was allowed to take a job as an industrial worker. Kendeh and his wife, with their three minor children, were deported to the remote village of Kamutpuszta in southern Hungary. The local authorities assigned them one room in a farm building in which to live. They were permitted to move freely only within a circumference of four miles. When one of the children became ill, the father was not allowed to get a physician because he lived further than the four miles away. The parish pastor helped him, but he was called to account for it by the bishop.

The leadership of the church did not dare to render consolation or assistance to the thousands of innocent people who had been deported in such a manner. Bishop Dezséry even expressed his appreciation for the measures of the government. The church leadership also tried to demonstrate its loyalty to the rulers in other matters — for example, regarding the so-called voluntary "government bonds for peace" that took the savings of the poorer people in particular, who earned only minimal wages, or regarding certain foreign policy actions, such as protests in writing on behalf of Communists imprisoned in the West. The pastoral letter of the bishop, which was read from all pulpits on October 4, 1953, caused a great sensation since it mainly consisted of propaganda for collectivization by force.

In such a church there was no longer any room for Lajos Ordass. No congregation was able to invite a preacher or speaker without first notifying the authorities. That is why Ordass did not even have to be prohibited to speak. Whoever wanted to invite him for an evening with a congregation was told that it was not desirable. The church leadership even threatened with reprisals anyone who sought contact with Ordass. The pastor of the congregation where Ordass worshiped every Sunday was asked to urge Ordass discreetly to stay away from the services to avoid any relationship with members of the congregation. Fewer and fewer people dared to defy the prohibition of the church leadership.

His family also began to feel the consequences of this banishment. His son Barnabás studied theology in Sopron until the Theological Faculty was separated from the university, the dormitory confiscated, and the institution transferred to Budapest under the name "Theological

Academy." The leadership of the dormitory applied for and received permission to stay in Budapest with the approximately one hundred students of theology, except for four, among whom was Ordass's son. Barnabás was in the midst of his studies, but he had to live officially in Sopron. A benevolent police official helped him to get provisional permission to live in Budapest. But shortly before the end of his studies he was completely excluded from the study of theology.

A young pastor who wanted to marry Ordass's daughter was asked by Dean Miklós Pálfy to choose between marriage and service. When the political weather changed he was finally able to enter the ministry as well as to marry his fiancée.

Neither of the two verdicts against Ordass had affected his claim for his pension. But in order to receive the full pension he would have to apply for transfer into retirement. But he could not do so. He regarded both verdicts as illegal. If he applied for retirement they could say that he acknowledged his verdict as lawful. So he now received from the treasury of the church only one-third of his salary as a pastor, about 1,000 forint (then about $100). To be sure, the prospect was held out to him that the church would settle his financial situation by procuring a residence for him. But every time there was a prospect of an appropriate residence there were no means in the church treasury. Finally, a residence was assigned to him in a building that had once belonged to the house of deaconesses. Here, in the Márvány home for deaconnesses, he lived with his wife for twenty-seven years.

Few in the church had the courage to associate with him openly and with friendliness. It was simpler for fellow believers abroad, and they showed him often that he had not been forgotten. The president and general secretary of the Lutheran World Federation intervened repeatedly for just treatment of the former bishop. The Norwegian bishop, Eivind Berggrav, wrote a forceful letter to the church leadership, expressing his dismay about what had happened.

Even though there was usually no reaction to these advances from abroad, it became clear that the church leadership was not insensitive to the ideas that were expressed by sister churches abroad about the church in Hungary and Ordass's fate. This became especially evident in connection with the preparations for the assembly of the Lutheran World Federation in Hannover in 1952.

Ordass was, of course, invited to the assembly as vice president. A few weeks before the assembly, Bishops Vető and Dezséry asked Ordass for a conversation and visited him at home. Later in the same day, Ordass produced a transcript of the conversation and the reproaches that had been brought up.

It was his fault, so Vető said, that the Lutheran Church in Hungary was no longer receiving aid from the sister churches abroad. Ordass responded that the reason was rather that a Hungarian court had ascertained in 1948 that the church had "assets" at its disposal abroad. Perhaps the sister churches wanted to demonstrate that this was not so.

But the main concern of the bishops was to show that "Western circles" had now "yoked the World Federation to the service of Western politics." Thus it would be unfortunate if Ordass would permit himself to be elected to a second term. Such a move could have very calamitous consequences for the Lutheran Church in Hungary and also for Ordass himself. About the kind of "calamitous consequences" no answer was given by the visitors. Both visitors wanted Ordass to indicate in writing in advance that he did not wish to be a candidate for a position of leadership of the World Federation. Otherwise, the Lutheran Church in Hungary would be forced to leave the Federation.

Ordass retorted that the members of the Executive Committee were elected according to the principle of rotation so that a delegate from another minority church automatically would take the position. The kind of letter the bishops desired would only make him look uninformed about the unwritten rules of the World Federation.

During the assembly in Hannover, the question was raised from the floor why Ordass was not present. Dezséry responded that his absence was due to the fact that he had not applied for an exit permit. Actually the president of the World Federation, Bishop Nygren, had applied for such a permit for Ordass and immediately received a negative reply. In the opening worship service, Bishop Lilje mentioned in prayer "the brothers and sisters who were not allowed to come to the assembly." Although Ordass was not mentioned by name, both Hungarian bishops demanded that Bishop Lilje publicly retract his statement, which, of course, he refused to do. On the contrary, a sentiment of solidarity with Ordass was expressed repeatedly and in various ways.

Guests from sister churches abroad also showed during visits to Hungary that he had not been forgotten. These guests completely ignored Bishop Dezséry's prohibition to visit Ordass. One of them was the Swedish pastor and Ordass's former fellow student Daniel Cederberg; he evaded the spy in his hotel and visited Ordass twice early in the morning. Dezséry had spoken of Cederberg's intended visit to Hungary at his conversation with Ordass before the assembly: "I told Cederberg that he should visit you, but he refused." Ordass disclosed nothing.

Financially, the years 1949 to 1956 were a difficult time for the Ordass family. All the children were still at home, and one-third of a pastor's salary was not sufficient even to support the parents. Both made every effort to earn more income. They succeeded in acquiring a knitting machine to produce sweaters, stockings, and woolen gloves. Later they tried their hand at leather goods. Then they moved to the production of sandals made of corn leaves. As he later put it grinningly: "It was fashionable for a time to wear a scarf knitted by Bishop Ordass. But this fashion, like other fashion trends, soon passed."

Of greatest benefit to the family was the garden at the outskirts of the city that Ordass was able to lease for three years. Although it did not earn much money, it supplied the family with vegetables and fruit. Activity in the open air outside the city was good for him. But in the fall of 1955 heart troubles forced him to end his work in the garden.

On one occasion his knowledge of Swedish almost helped him to earn money. A governmental firm in the clothing industry was looking for an interpreter. He was allowed to submit a trial translation and to present himself for an interview. But various questions during the interview led him to surmise that the decision lay in different hands. The speedy answer he was promised never arrived.

Although literary work and translations of Scandinavian literature did not yield any material gain, they were a source of great delight. Ordass could also write down now all that he had thought about in the prison in Vác, the meditations and short stories about "people on my way." He deepened his knowledge of Icelandic in order to translate a significant work of Icelandic literature from the seventeenth century, Hallgrímur Pétursson's *Passíusálmar (Lenten Hymns)* of 1666. Shortly after the war, a friend had given him a copy of the Icelandic text, but he had not had the time then to study its language and content. Now he had the opportunity to study the literature on the topic. He was fascinated by the fact that the poet lived on for the population of the "island of sagas" three hundred years after his death. Because Hallgrímur's life had also been marked by various sufferings, he felt particularly attracted to this personality. He also had come to know the archbishop of Iceland, Sigurgeir Sigurdsson, at the assembly in Lund and had deepened his friendship with him during a preaching tour in Denmark.

It is said that Ordass prayed ardently for the gift of poetry during his translation of the Lenten hymns, a request he wished to make only once and never trouble God with such a prayer again. Not only was his prayer heard, but he also translated other Scandinavian hymns in poetic form.

The story of Christ's passion had a special place in his daily Bible reading. The manuscript of his own Lenten meditations, *At the Foot of the Cross,* arrived in a roundabout way in Minneapolis in the middle 1950s, was translated into English, and was printed there in 1956. This book, too, shows how the image of the suffering Savior in the church of Torzsa had made an indelible impression on him. When he now in his solitude also learned "neo-Norwegian," the second official language of Norway, he was particularly drawn to the Lenten hymn of Johannes Barstad, and he translated it into Hungarian: "Be still, oh so still, Jesus suffers. . . ."

Ordass was probably unaware what great service such work rendered to his church, which he dearly loved. He attended the worship service in the congregation of Budahegyvidék, his place of residence, every Sunday. Apart from this, he was forced to view the events in the church as a spectator.

The 1948 agreement between the government and the Lutheran Church was to ensure the obligatory teaching of religion in the schools. But within a year this teaching was declared by law to be elective. The troubles for parents never ceased when they wanted to enroll their children for the teaching of religion within the legal time limit of two days. In the middle of the 1950s only fifty students participated in the Lutheran teaching of religion in Budapest, even though about 60,000 Lutherans lived in the city. According to the 1948 agreement, the church was to keep two of its gymnasium schools. But Bishop Dezséry found the financial burden for the church to be too great and asked the government to take over the schools, without any consultation with church authorities. The position of the Theological Faculty was also ensured in the agreement. Nevertheless, the Faculty was separated from the university a year and a half later.

It did not take long until the diaconical work of the church also began to suffer. There were three homes for deaconesses. Fébé (Phoebe) was the largest of these homes; it contained homes for the elderly, for students, and for children, along with a printing press — twenty-three various institutions altogether and nearly two hundred deaconesses. A government regulation dissolved the home for deaconesses, together with most Roman Catholic monasteries, and the wearing of ecclesiastical garb was prohibited. Half of the institutions belonging to Fébé were taken over by the government; the other half were transformed into homes for retired employees of the church and for handicapped children. In this area the church was still permitted to take responsibility.

In 1951, a governmental church administration, the "State Office for Religious Affairs," was instituted, presided over by the previously mentioned István Kossa as "church minister." Gradually, the office gained effective control over the churches. The editor of the only existing Lutheran paper, *Evangélikus Élet*, had to appear there every week in order to receive his "imprimatur." Bishops were ordered to come there when there was a complaint against a pastor or when a personnel question was on the agenda.

The 1948 agreement stated that a permanent board, formed by church and state together, should review any new laws affecting the churches. Now, however, laws and regulations came into effect without any opportunity for the church to state an opinion.

Many faithful servants of the church appeared as rays of hope in this gloomy picture. They quietly continued to do their work in the congregations. The awakening that had swept the country in the 1940s now yielded a rich harvest. But one could not draw public attention to oneself. Much conscientious theological work was also quietly done. These were the fruits that the "dismissed" bishop could view with gratitude.

22. Thaw in Hungary

JOSEPH STALIN died March 5, 1953. An obituary appeared as the lead article in *Evangélikus Élet,* expressing "the deep sorrow" of the Hungarian people about the loss.

> Josef Stalin, the wise leader of all peace-loving people, is dead. But his work, his mental and moral heritage, remains a glowing example for all of us and for the world.

It would soon become evident that a whole epoch had passed with his death. For the time being one could only watch the signs of an internal power struggle behind the scenes. Leaders and members of the government were exchanged. Titoists (followers of Marshal Tito) were rehabilitated, and loyal followers of Moscow were arrested. The famous speech of Khrushchev at the Twentieth Party Congress in Moscow in February 1956 was, of course, not published. But it was followed by a thaw in the Soviet Union and in the rest of the East European countries.

In the spring of 1956 it was possible to speak more freely. People who had been sentenced to long prison terms were suddenly prematurely released. Already in 1955 the Roman Catholic archbishop Grösz was released from prison; he was allowed to take over the presidency of the college of bishops in the spring of 1956. Cardinal Mindszenty was permitted to exchange his prison cell for house arrest. Even László Rajk, who was executed in 1952, was now to be rehabilitated. For the first time in nine years the association of writers was allowed to have free elections. The previous president, József Darvas, was no longer elected at all. But it took a long time before members of the Lutheran Church could breathe more freely. The leadership of the church, however, obeyed these new signals as they had the old.

The annual assembly of the Central Committee of the World Council of Churches was planned for the summer of 1956 in the vacation town of Galyatető in the Mátra mountains of Hungary. The leadership in the State Office for Church Affairs was anticipating this assembly with some discomfort, for they were very sensitive to church opinion abroad even though they maintained the appearance of indifference. It had become clear to them that the government's treatment of Ordass was causing them a headache. It was increasingly uncomfortable to be confronted with the questions of the leaders of the Lutheran World Federation about their former vice president, and to have to admit that he made a bare living with only a third of his salary as a pastor.

Accordingly, one day Ordass received an invitation to the State Office for Church Affairs to discuss "his pension problem." Ordass responded in writing that he knew nothing about a "pension problem." A representative of the office received the same reply when he visited Ordass. The director of the office, János Horváth, appeared on the same day, together with a young deputy, Imre Miklós. They told Ordass that he could count on a regular pension as well as an additional payment of 25,000 forint, then a substantial sum, if he agreed to the pension.

Ordass declared that he could not accept such an offer. He did not demand a pension but rather justice. He said that he was innocent of the charges of which he had been convicted by a people's court, and that the church had committed a series of illegalities when it dismissed him from his office. All this had to be put in order. But he was not the only one who had been treated unlawfully. The two pastors Kendeh and Keken had experienced similar injustice, and they, too, had a right to justice. These were the matters that had to be negotiated, not the question of a pension or a later payment.

János Horváth promised to think about the matter. Two weeks later he told Ordass that the verdict of the people's court would be examined. It would be more difficult to revise the ecclesiastical verdict.

A further step was made when the foreign guests had arrived in Galyatető. Bishop Lilje, President Fry, and the General Secretary of the World Council Dr. Visser 't Hooft made immediate contact with the governmental church office. On August 3 there was a first meeting of the three guests with Horváth and Miklós as representatives of the government and Dezséry and Vető as representatives of the church. Ordass was also invited. The General Secretary of the Lutheran World Federation, Dr. Lund-Quist, was also included in the negotiations. After several sessions it was agreed that Ordass should take a professorship at the Theological Academy. The possibility was left open for him to resume his episcopal office again at some later time.

Ordass was not very satisfied with this solution. A rehabilitation should have brought with it reinstatement to the episcopal office. Moreover, his heavy load of work in the church for many years had prevented him from qualifying for the theological teaching office. But the foreign negotiation partners urged him to accept the agreement.

Shortly thereafter the guests left the country. The State Office for Church Affairs took the necessary steps to promote his case. But very little happened in the church. One could read in foreign newspapers that the rehabilitation of Ordass was imminent. But *Evangélikus Élet* had not said a single word about it. On the contrary, Bishop Dezséry used a meeting of seniors on August 24 to criticize Ordass sharply in the presence of members of the governmental church office. He had also invited to this meeting a number of younger pastors, who participated in the conversation and characterized Ordass as reactionary, proud, and not at all worthy of the pastoral office. It seemed as if János Horváth was right: Ordass might, no doubt, be rehabilitated by the government, but there would be problems with it in the church.

But the freer intellectual climate became apparent in ever wider circles and gradually also among Lutheran pastors. At gatherings and assemblies resolutions and decisons were made. Pastors and congregations who wanted to do away with what was old haunted the leadership of the church. They wanted the rehabilitation of Ordass and other pastors whom the church had treated unjustly.

Gradually churches abroad also became impatient and asked about the realization of the agreement that had been published abroad already in the beginning of August.

The Supreme Court of Hungary rescinded the verdict of Lajos Ordass on October 5, and he was "acquitted of the charges, for lack of violating the law." Only after the church leadership had received this decision did the regular court of the church convene. It rescinded the verdict of the special court of April 1, 1950, "because of formal and substantial mistakes." Ordass was acquitted "of all legal consequences." His "full rehabilitation" was decided, and it was certified that "the ecclesiastical case of discipline against him is to be regarded as null and void." Moreover, it was noted that Ordass was entitled to "moral and material" reparation.

In the next issue of *Evangélikus Élet* Ordass was again mentioned, for the first time in six years. His rehabilitation was reported, along with a commentary.

On October 14, 1956, he preached his first public sermon in eight years. The worshipers filled not only the church of Budahegyvidék but also the streets nearby. The sermon was published in the next issue of *Evangélikus Élet*. His sermon text was the text for the twentieth Sunday after Trinity, Matthew 22, the parable of the royal wedding feast:

> The Bible speaks often of Christ as the bridegroom and the congregation or the individual Christian as his bride. Is this exaggerated, or only a poetic, empty word? No, the reality even surpasses the parable.
>
> I am to proclaim God's word here to a congregation so large that I cannot see every person, a congregation whose heart thirsts for the Word of God. I have the feeling that God forces me not only to explicate the substance of the biblical messages but also to bear witness to the joy of Christian life as I have experienced it.
>
> When two people want to get married they often say to each other: "You are my one and all! I love you until death, forever." I have heard the same words in my life with my Lord and Savior. He said to me, his unworthy servant: "You are my one and all." I know that he said that to me in the moment when I wanted to give up. He said it as if I were the only human being on earth. I have heard it from him: "I love you until death, eternally!" When there was no human hand I could hold, he firmly held mine. To him the cross, to me his peace. To him death, to me his fruit: life.

At the end of the sermon he referred to the servants who had been sent out to invite the wedding guests:

> Today I am the servant of the king. I have delivered the invitation. You may forget the exact words. But keep in mind: God is on the way to see whether you cling to your dirty clothes. I give you good advice: accept the invitation.

Overnight his residence became a place of pilgrimage. People who had not visited him for years and who had even warned others against doing so came to congratulate him. He was not very pleased with this mass migration, but he hoped that his conciliatory stance might ease the conscience of one or more persons. He refused the offered reparation, which would have had to be paid from the already meager treasury of the church. He was very pleased that the pastors Keken and Kendeh had also been installed again in their offices.

One week later, on October 24, he was to give his first lecture on "Luther research in Scandinavia" at the Theological Academy.

23. Once Again, a New Beginning

In the same issue of *Evangélikus Élet* that reported the rehabilitation of Bishop Lajos Ordass there was also an extensive report about a convention of seniors that had just been concluded. At the convention Bishop Vető had presented a "twenty-four-point reform program" by order of the total church leadership.

The program held out the prospect of addressing all matters of suspected unjust measures against workers in the church. Vacant positions of seniors and other important offices were to be filled immediately. Congregations would be able to express their opinions, as before, on the election of pastors. Pastors who had been retired would again have the right to render service temporarily. Mission work and spiritual retreats would be allowed again. The church leadership would no longer have the exclusive right to make decisons that affected the whole church. *Evangélikus Élet* would be subject to a special editorial committee, and the circle of those involved in its publication would be expanded. There would again be the possibility of protest when local authorities tampered with the instruction of religion and of confirmands. Thus a concession had been made after eight years that there had been abuse, neglect, and injustice. The way was paved for a promising new beginning.

Those responsible for these concessions certainly made an effort to save face. According to the words of Ernő Mihályfi, "the legitimate organs of the church had helped the church on the basis of the new law to a victory of the truth and to the rehabilitation of the condemned." According to Bishop Vető, the rehabilitation and the visit of the World

ONCE AGAIN, A NEW BEGINNING

Council of Churches, as well as other events, showed that "our church essentially had gone the right way during the last years."

Ordass was not present at the session, but he gladly took note of the report; the time now demanded not attributions of guilt or emphasis on questions of form, said Ordass, but reforms that must be put in place without hesitation. Moreover, unlawfully appointed officials gradually realized that their time was over. Pastors who had taken over the offices of other deposed colleagues withdrew, one after another. The general Secretary of the church, Károly Grünvalszky, submitted his letter of resignation on October 18. Already in the early summer János Horváth had told Ordass in confidence that the authorities wanted to separate themselves from Dezséry so that the road would be open for Ordass to resume his office.

On the day when *Professor* Ordass was to give his first lecture, students and teachers stayed away from the universities throughout Hungary. The day before, on October 23, massive student demonstrations took place in the capital. They started with banners demanding a better order of stipends. But soon they turned to political slogans like "Russians go home." The president of the Communist Party, Rákosi, had already long before been deposed by the rulers in Moscow and was spending an undeserved vacation at the Black Sea. His successor in the party, Ernő Gerő, did not assess the situation correctly. Shots were fired into the crowd, and the demonstrations changed into an armed rebellion. The street fights lasted several days and caused much loss of human life and damage to property. The iron grip of the party diminished, and the crowds rejoiced. Even the highest leaders in Moscow behaved as if they accepted the fact that a new era had begun in Hungary.

This situation also accelerated the renewal of the Lutheran Church beyond all expectation. On October 30, László Dezséry submitted his letter of resignation from the episcopal office in the southern district in favor of its legitimate incumbent Lajos Ordass. In his letter he asked that God would bless the service of Ordass.

Although the general strike had shut down all public transportation in Budapest, the large church at Deák-tér was filled to capacity when Ordass presided at the church service there again for the first time on October 31. This day, Reformation Day, was always one of the great festival days of the Protestant churches in Hungary. Now Lutheran parishioners from the whole capital assembled to hear their bishop once again.

On Sunday, October 28, there had hardly been any worship services in the churches. Ordass, too, had been unable to deliver the sermon he had prepared for the worship service in the congregation of Zugló. So on Reformation Day he used the biblical text for that Sunday: the story of the unforgiving servant in Matthew 18. "Forgiveness gives life — hatred kills" was his topic. This theme hit home among his listeners, given the inflammatory atmosphere after the fall of the hated dictatorship. At the end of his sermon he referred to Jesus' appearance in the synagogue of Nazareth (Luke 4), the appropriate text for Reformation Day. "Now we need the gospel. God is the God of forgiveness."

Anyone who had expected to hear a "political" sermon that unreservedly paid homage to the uprising was disappointed. The emphasis of this sermon, right after the bloody reckoning with the old regime, was of a different sort.

One event followed hot on the heels of another. Bishop Vető also resigned. In his letter of resignation he wrote, among other things: "The power of demonic forces in our land and in our church has broken down before our eyes." He also declared that he would relinquish his tasks in the World Council of Churches. Like others, Ernő Mihályfi left Hungary already during the uprising because he was afraid that his leading position during the Stalin era would now cause him difficulties. Ordass called József Darvas and urged him to resign from his office of church inspector since his office was necessarily in conflict with his outlook on life. Darvas agreed and promised to resign.

At issue were no longer a few reforms but a complete upheaval of society. In the church Ordass was viewed as one who could give advice and leadership. His days were more than filled. One of the seniors asked him to pay a brief formal visit to Cardinal Mindszenty, who had been released from house arrest and had returned to Budapest. Ordass also prepared a "greeting" that was broadcast by Hungarian radio on November 2 in four languages: Hungarian, German, English, and Swedish. The greeting was broadcast in Sweden several times on the same day. In it Ordass said, among other things:

> Many difficult questions confront us in these days. Many have fallen in the fighting and many families have lost their breadwinner and supporter. We have many who are wounded and need care and medicine. There is much damage to buildings and personal belongings. In the name of Jesus Christ, come and help us! We want to do our

best, through our church institutions, to help all those in need. May God bless you all!

Already within a few days relief shipments were sent by the Lutheran World Federation and other institutions. All those who brought such relief connected the trip, whenever possible, with a visit to Ordass.

Quick action was necessary in many areas. Already on Saturday, November 3, Ordass convened all the pastors and professors of theology whom he was able to contact despite the lack of mail service and telephone connections. A surprising number came, almost fifty persons.

A series of provisional decisions were made in order to "restart the church administration's motor." Bishop Túróczy was requested to administer the northern diocese for the time being. Some were made responsible for the distribution of information in the church, others for the distribution of relief shipments; one person was asked to serve as editor of *Evangélikus Élet,* and another to serve temporarily as general secretary of church administration. A letter was sent to all seniors requesting them to resign from their offices. They had all been "elected" according to the way of the people's democracy — that is, simply installed by the church leadership — and it was now up to them to run for office together with other candidates in a free election.

These and other provisionary decisions were later confirmed by the legal organs of the church. But before that could take place, new dramatic events closed in on the Hungarian people. On Sunday, November 4, Soviet tanks rolled into the country, bringing quick disillusionment after the frenzy of liberty. It seemed inevitable that the clocks would be turned back. No one in the Lutheran Church could predict if the decisions of November 3 would remain in force. In the southern diocese the leaders selected by and dependent on Dezséry were still in place. They were now to approve his resignation. The session was anticipated with a certain tension. But no one spoke a word in Dezséry's defense, as Ordass observed with surprise, almost with a certain disappointment.

The surprise, indeed joy, was even greater when the State Office of Church Affairs accepted the new situation in the Lutheran Church. Already three weeks after the Soviet intervention the first dialogue took place between Ordass and János Horváth. Horváth accepted the resignations of Dezséry, Mihályfi, and Vető without hesitation. He himself would contact József Darvas in order to confirm his resignation. Horváth also declared that from now on registrations for religious instruction no longer needed to be reported to the authorities. This meant that students who participated in such instruction no longer needed to fear discrimination. Horváth even agreed that the two gymnasiums which Dezséry had handed over to the government without authorization would be returned to the church. In addition, Ordass, and all other church delegates, would be allowed to leave the country in order to attend the assembly of the Lutheran World Federation in Minneapolis.

It seemed almost too good to be true. But in any case, Ordass and his co-workers had a welcome breathing space in which to begin to revive life in the church, which had lost much of its vitality during the Stalinist era. This was no easy task in a land that was still paralyzed by strikes and where there was prohibition of assembly until the next spring (although not prohibition of worship or church assemblies). Many buildings were in ruins, though fewer than after the war. But rebuilding the spiritual life of the churches was needed more desperately than the reconstruction of buildings. The most important thing was restoring the church's credibility in the eyes of the congregations, who had had their fill of political circular letters and slogans, and in the eyes of the political leaders, who had become accustomed to church leaders who always adjusted themselves to whomever had power for the moment.

At the end of January 1957, the general secretary of the Lutheran World Federation, Dr. Lund-Quist, together with the secretary for minority churches, the Danish pastor Mogens Zeuthen, visited Hungary. The latter had studied in Sopron before the war and spoke Hungarian very well. The guests met with the leaders of the governmental church office and discovered that they had confidence in Ordass as the leader of the Lutheran Church. Lund-Quist also received confirmation that a delegation of six, led by Ordass, had been given permission to travel to Minneapolis. Lund-Quist returned to Geneva after a few days, but Zeuthen stayed for another week and was present at the reinstallation of Bishop Túróczy. Túróczy had lost his office in 1952 when the four church districts had been combined into two. After the resignation of Vető, the congregations of the northern diocese again elected him as their bishop. Governmental representatives were also present at his installation.

Zeuthen brought a Volkswagen car as a gift to the church. Now it was easier for Ordass to conduct his episcopal service of visitation in congregations and with pastors. Clergy conventions were not hindered by the prohibition of assemblies. Ordass visited all eight seniors within a month and got to meet almost every pastor in his diocese. Both Ordass and the pastors drew consolation and encouragement from these contacts. The pastors were full of hope and plans, despite all the difficulties. Once again youth work had begun here and there. Participation in religious instruction increased from an average of 30 percent to 80 percent, in some cases even 100 percent.

The life of the church during the first months of 1957 generated hope for a period of blessed and fruitful labor.

24. Minneapolis, 1957

ON JULY 31, 1957, the *United States* left the French port of Le Havre for New York. Aboard was the Hungarian delegation for the world assembly of the Lutheran World Federation. The journey had begun with some nervousness. The church's relation to the ruling political powers had become once again more tense. The original composition of the delegation had not been approved by the governmental church office. Two members had to be exchanged. But the number of capable pastors and theologians was sufficiently large that Ordass gave in and made the substitutions rather than risk the whole journey.

It was not the first time since his rehabilitation that he had been abroad. In March, the Conference of European Churches convened in Liselund, Denmark. The governmental church office had insisted that Ordass attend. A surprising number of East European churches were represented, among them the Lutheran churches of Esthonia and Latvia. That was sensational at that time.

At a visit with Bishop Fuglsang Damgaard in Copenhagen Ordass had the pleasure of meeting the widow of the poet-pastor Kaj Munk. She had come from Vedersö on purpose to meet the man who had translated several of her husband's plays.

Late in the spring a Hungarian delegation of eight had traveled to Salzerbad, Austria, to participate in a preparatory conference for the assembly in Minneapolis. Here Ordass met for the first time in ten years his younger friend Vilmos Vajta, who had been entrusted in the meantime with the direction of the department of theology of the Lutheran World Federation. They had last seen each other during the founding assembly of the Federation in 1947 in Lund. At the conferences in Liselund and Salzerbad Ordass could catch his breath, as it were, before he journeyed for a month to the United States.

At the port of New York, Paul Empie awaited the Hungarian group. He had been general secretary of the National Lutheran Council in the United States since 1948, and Ordass knew him from his previous visit in New York. They had several long discussions in which Ordass could now hear about all the details and see documents that showed the great efforts of many church leaders to secure his release and rehabilitation. Even though all the attempts had failed, when Ordass heard all this from Empie and saw all his archive materials he felt great gratitude for the support of this large sisterly community. It was less pleasant to note as well that certain leading individuals in his own church and some Hungarians in the United States had made efforts to undermine his credibility abroad.

The Hungarian delegates traveled to Minneapolis on various roads. Ordass was to stop in Northfield, Minnesota, in order to attend the session of the Executive Committee.

The opening worship service of the Assembly was held in Central Hall, a convention center that held twelve thousand people. Ordass had never addressed as many people as he did in that service, which was televised for several churches in the area. Directly or indirectly, about thirty thousand people were present at the opening ceremony.

His sermon was simultaneously sad and visionary. The topic of the Assembly was "Christ liberates and unites." Ordass preached on the words of Jesus in John 12 about the grain of wheat that must fall in the earth to bring forth life. He spoke of from what and for what Jesus' death liberates his people, and also of how Jesus' death unites his followers with God and links disciples with each other. One participant in the worship service reported that when Ordass carefully touched upon the experiences of his time in prison, a movement went through the congregation like an electric shock:

> An elderly disciple of Jesus now speaks to you. He wants to conclude this official sermon with a personal testimony about his Lord and Savior. He would like to say how often he has experienced already in his life the forgiving grace of Christ. When he had to experience being imprisoned, he was still able to be with Christ in royal freedom in the truest sense of the word. What happiness to have been allowed

such freedom! How wonderful was the fruit of the death of Christ then, when the world offered only bitterness.

Many experiences marked the two weeks of the Assembly — meetings with old friends, new acquaintances with representatives from many countries and churches. All of it left a deep impression on him, since for eight years he had lived almost cut off from the world around him. But what pleased him even more than being together with old and new friends was the work of the World Federation itself. The breadth of the work described in the reports impressed him since he came from a church whose circle of operation was very limited. He was fascinated by plans and visions for future work. His enthusiasm was contagious for the other members of the Hungarian delegation, as can be seen in the reports that were written after their return.

A Hungarian eucharistic worship service was a highpoint of Ordass's stay in the United States. According to his desire and after a discussion with General Secretary Lund-Quist, the worship service took place within the program of the General Assembly. Ordass counted on the presence of some Hungarian Lutherans among the many delegates and visitors from the United States and from various countries. His wish was that they should really encounter each other and experience true community at the table of the Lord.

He imagined beforehand a small group of perhaps twenty to twenty-five people, and he was glad to think that he would be able to share with them God's Word and the Lord's Supper. Great was his surprise when he saw, almost with alarm, that the Hungarian worship service was to take place in the almost fully occupied Central Church, with two hundred to three hundred participants.

Not everyone participated in the eucharist. But besides the Hungarian guests he saw familiar faces from many countries. There was a delegate from Indonesia, who happened to celebrate his birthday on this day, and the well-known resistance fighter Provost Grüber from Berlin with his wife; Ruth Wick, the faithful travel companion of the Hungarian delegation in the United States. He was particularly moved when he saw the widow of his good friend Michelfelder, the Former General Secretary of the World Federation, whose grave site he also visited.

The majority of those present did not understand a word of Ordass's sermon. But he read the text from John 11:28, in which Martha says to her sister Mary, "The Teacher is here and is calling for you," in English. Most of the participants also did not understand much of the Hungarian eucharistic liturgy, which had a special feature: the confession of sins with the participants' responses to five questions of confession is part of the liturgy itself. Even though the words of the prayers and of the answers were incomprehensible to many in this worshiping congregation, Ordass said later that Jesus Christ was present for all with his grace and his blessing in the holy meal.

Ordass was again elected to be a member of the Executive Committee and also to be first vice president of the Committee. Franklin C. Fry, his intimate friend, became president. One of the other two vice presidents was his former fellow student Bo Giertz. Ordass was very grateful that his service for Lutheranism in the world was still desired. He could not know then that he would not be allowed to participate in a single session of the Committee during this term.

Ordass was asked to offer a greeting at the concluding service of the Assembly in a stadium in Minneapolis; 128,000 people were present.

25. "Is the Informer More Reliable than the Bishop?"

THE RETURN home to the great and small problems of the daily round was almost disillusioning.

Already in the course of the spring the relationship between the churches and the governmental church office had begun to deteriorate. The brief period of harmony had been only an intermediate state and could no longer be reconciled with the political situation in the country. The new regime under the rule of János Kádár dealt with the rebels very carefully in the beginning. Councils of laborers and even "revolutionary councils" were allowed to endure in factories and professional organizations and to appear as negotiation partners of the government. But after a government delegation returned from a visit to Moscow in March of 1957, a new wave of terror moved over the country, and the government's attitude toward the church changed again.

Some Lutheran pastors happened to be caught in the limelight because they had played an active role during the uprising. Eight of them were arrested and sent to labor camps. Ordass tried to negotiate for each one's release, but the majority of them had to wait the usual six months before their case was brought to trial. The Communist media became negative toward the church again. The editor of a local newspaper sharply attacked Ordass after a visitation. Ordass responded in a letter, calling attention to the many inaccuracies in the article. The editor had Ordass's letter printed and added a sarcastic commentary. Ordass was glad just to have a chance to speak. The readers could at least form their own opinion. Soon the time would come when newspapers did not publish any corrections.

The leader of the Office for Church Affairs, János Horváth, was not satisfied that some of the seniors who had come into office under Bishop Deszséry had not been reelected but had been replaced by others. He accused the bishops of having manipulated the election, as was customary in the people's democracy!

The governmental church office again demanded participation in meetings that were to demonstrate "national unity" through common participation of Communists and non-Communists. Ordass appeared at a convention of the "Patriotic People's Front" and was asked to speak. When he took the liberty of emphasizing that the church had its own, critical voice in such a context, he was most rudely corrected by the minister of the interior, Ferenc Münnich. Ordass thought it was no longer fitting to appear in such a context. Nevertheless, he was designated as a president of the People's Front, without being asked.

The governmental church office demanded from the Lutheran Church the establishment of a "peace council," which was to be incorporated into the respective governmental organ. Ordass and his coworkers knew quite well that these organs could be abused. But they regarded the matter of peace so important that they did establish a Lutheran peace council after solid theological reflection.

At the end of March 1957 the Presidential Council issued a legal ordinance according to which all candidates who were assigned higher offices in any church had to be confirmed by the authorities. This ordinance was to be valid retroactively as of October 1, 1956.

János Horváth called Ordass early in the morning of the day when the ordinance was to be published. He wanted to inform Ordass about the ordinance and assure him "that the retroactive power of the ordinance would, of course, not apply to the Lutheran Church since everything was in order there." But in fact the entire Lutheran leadership was taken out of office during the next sixteen months, by authority of this ordinance.

Although Horváth had given assurance that the ordinance would not apply to the Lutheran Church, the bishop thought it important to express his deviating opinion on specific points in writing. He thought that the Agreement of 1948 had provided the continual validity of church laws. According to these laws, congregations had the right to elect their own pastors, bishops, and other officers. Moreover, the Agreement had determined that new chuch laws had to be prepared by a common committee of church and state. This committee had not even been established during the eight years since the Agreement had been signed.

Ordass's written response was not answered, and no common committee was established. From March 1957 until 1988, no one could be nominated for the office of bishop or the position of professor of theology unless his candidacy was approved by the authorities. But only one candidate for each position was approved (in 1987/88 two), and this candidate was then "elected." Gradually, this practice was extended to the designation of seniors and even pastors of more significant congregations.

When Ordass returned from Minneapolis at the end of September, so many delicate problems had accumulated that he felt it necessary to have a comprehensive discussion of unsettled questions with the State Office of Church Affairs. But János Horváth was on a study trip to the People's Republic of China, and his deputy, Imre Miklós, advised Ordass to summarize his comments in writing. This led to a letter of twelve pages, which waited for Horváth after he returned from his China trip.

Ordass stressed in the beginning of the letter that he had no intention of making available a list of church grievances. He knew that he was at one with the president of the church office regarding the common basis — namely, the Agreement of 1948.

The letter then mentioned personnel questions. The lawful election of persons to fill positions long vacant had become difficult and impeded despite the suspension of the prohibition of assembly. There was uncertainty regarding the application of the governmental "regulation that a subsequent confirmation of the vacancy or filling of certain offices is necessary." For the president had told Ordass personally "that, keeping our church in mind, this ordinance should not apply to the legal regulations of the previous fall." Ordass then firmly rejected the reproach that his church "disregards progressive church officers, deliberately and with slow speed" and furthers "the placing of reactionaries in higher positions."

The next topic in the letter was the church press. There had been unanimity about the following: "the church lets the press do its work by keeping in mind the interest of the church and does nothing that might cause unrest from the viewpoint of the authority of the state." Nevertheless, the representatives of the governmental church office increasingly intervened and demanded "a higher degree of 'progress' from the editors and co-workers." "This is the place where there is the deepest opposition between our points of views," wrote Ordass. He stressed that politicalization of the church press would raise the "inevitable question among church people whether the freedom of the church is in danger. . . . This fact is not only true for the members of the church who live in the country, but also for the echo of our press in the rest of the world." Ordass then spoke of his task as the editor of *Church Press*, published together with the Reformed Church. He wrote, among other things:

> Mr. President! I urge you to have confidence in me that my judgment is better than that of the appropriate functionary in the governmental church office as to what belongs to the church press. For I am responsible for the church and care about its credibility. . . . What I say generally about the effect of the church press is in the highest degree true for the *Church Press*. I have to say that this branch of our press service has completely lost its credibility.

Ordass concluded that this situation could not serve the best interests of the government.

He then referred to his engagement in the Patriotic People's Front. He said that the deputy director of the governmental church office had suggested his entry into the national presidency of the People's Front. Now he wanted to be free "to resign from this office as he had accepted it, listening to the voice of his conviction."

A further topic was the church's connections abroad. Ordass wrote with pleasure about the freedom that had been granted in this context: the journey to Minneapolis, and so on. But there were "disturbances" and disturbing questions. Recently the government of Hungary had arranged for an exchange of visits between Hungary and the church authorities in the German Democratic Republic. But the church authorities in Hungary had not been informed, and the arrival of guests from Germany had been totally unexpected. Furthermore, permits for recreational travels of pastors and their wives, which had been well substantiated by the church, had been arbitrarily denied. A pastor, about whom the governmental church office received the report "that he did not relate well to the people's democracy," was not permitted to travel for a vacation to Finland, even though his bishop had very warmly recommended him. Ordass asked here whether "in the matter of attaining information the informer, unknown to me and obviously not benevolent, carries more weight than the bishop of the church?"

At the end of his letter Ordass finally took up the delicate topic of arrests and referred to the related question of the tense situation and undercurrent of mistrust in the whole country. He wrote of his astonishment at the hypocrisy that has resulted. "Indeed, I am astonished by the realization that people say something different in their public speaking than in private conversations. It is painful for me to have to discover that I am living among people with two souls. Their interest makes them say something different than what is their opinion." This ambivalence is even directed toward the rulers. "Do the authorities know that even those who demonstrate cooperation and unity are against them?" His conscience would not let him be quiet; he had to say this, "even though I know that it may be dangerous if you misunderstand me."

After he had reported about the specific case of an arrested village pastor who had been ill-treated by the police and now had the "halo of a hero" in the village, he concluded the letter in this way:

> Great and little things I have mixed. Perhaps the picture I wanted to compose becomes alive this way. I wanted to depict some outlines of the difficulties I see in the life of the country, but especially in the relationship between church and state. I have held in writing to what I used to do in our face-to-face conversations: to speak bluntly and openly. Expressing my joy over your happy return, I cordially greet you, Mr. President.

Candidly, but in a moderate tone, Ordass had described a series of questions in his letter that he thought important and worthy of discussion. Before he sent the letter he read it to some friends. The friends found his description correct but thought, as he did himself, that he would run the risk of another arrest and trial with this letter.

He mailed the letter on October 25, 1957. He could not do otherwise.

26. Deposed a Second Time

THE RESPONSE from the governmental church office came after about two weeks. Ordass was invited to discuss the open questions between church and state. But János Horváth insisted on naming the persons who would represent the church. Ordass felt compelled to protest against this attack. He believed that church law must be followed in nominating a church delegation. And in the end the nominations were done that way.

When the delegation of four arrived at the location for the negotiations on November 12, they encountered a governmental delegation of whom five belonged to the church: the former bishops József Szabó amd Lajos Vető, the theology professor Miklós Pálfy, the pastor Ádám Mekis, and Károly Grünvalszky. Pálfy had been active in the so-called peasant party since the end of the war: this party worked closely with the Communists. Mekis belonged to the seniors who had not been reelected in the spring of 1957, and Grünvalszky had resigned his office of general secretary of the church before the uprising. Horváth had invited these men to the session. Ordass wondered with what kind of emotions they sat at the negotiation table, for they should have known that their assignment was not authorized by the church.

Horváth stressed that the church existed in a Socialist state and had to accept this reality. The government would adhere to the Agreement of 1948 and would guarantee religious liberty. Indeed, it even granted the church financial support. That is why the church owed it to the government to place at its disposal its resources and energies. In this regard, the Lutheran Church, its leadership and press, had been too passive. One could not, of course, speak of direct resistance against the government, but, alluding to a Bible saying, Horváth said: "Whoever is not with us is against us!" Horváth used hard language, with no signs of compromise, and made it clear that the failure of these negotiations would lead "to a very uncomfortable situation for the church." In an adversary situation the church "could no longer count on any advantages."

Some members of the church in the state's delegation also spoke. Their language was more cautious, but it was evident that they acknowledged the demands of Horváth to be correct.

Regarding the personnel questions, the authorities desired the reappointment of Bishop Vető as well as the two inspectors Mihályfi and Darvas. There were also demands for changes in the leadership of the church administration, of the church press, and of the Theological Academy, as well as for new appointments in a series of pastoral offices. Fifteen concrete demands were made in the course of the discussion.

Ordass responded by calling attention to the fact that the offices mentioned had been filled very recently, and that this had been done according to valid law and the regulations of the church. This meeting should not at all be used to decide the filling of pastoral offices. According to a centuries-old tradition, the order of the Lutheran Church prescribes that pastors be elected exclusively by the congregations.

In his notes about the negotiations Ordass observed that at this stage of the discussion his remarks released a storm on the other side of the table. In a most agitated way Horváth declared that this was not a matter that was open for discussion, but an absolute demand on the part of the state. There was no longer room for negotiations.

The discussion was adjourned until the following week because, among other things, a visit from the leadership of the Lutheran World Federation, General Secretary Lund-Quist and the director of the theological department, Vilmos Vajta, was expected. Vajta was to see his homeland again for the first time after fifteen years. The guests visited congregations in Budapest and outside the capital. Vajta also gave lectures at the Theological Academy.

The negotiations continued after the departure of the guests but soon reached a dead end. Horváth blamed Ordass for the impasse. He also voiced his opinion that the rigid stance of the church delegation was due in part to the unfavorable influence of Lund-Quist and Vajta. So any connection with the church abroad must stop immediately. A commissioner would be appointed to supervise the activities of the Lutheran Church. He would have control over the correspondence with foreign countries, the episcopal circular letters, financial matters, and the activity of the Theological Academy. Every publication in the press would be severely censored. But the "religious activity" of the church, Horváth declared, would remain untouched.

When the state commissioner Károly Grnák appeared in the headquarters of the church a few days later, his first matter of business was the reappointment of General Inspector Mihályfi and of Bishop Lajos Vető. They were now confirmed as legitimate incumbents of the offices from which they had resigned in the fall of 1956. Bishop Túróczy, who had been lawfully elected in January of 1957 and installed in the presence of official representatives, submitted a written protest. But it was unsuccessful, and the bishop had to step aside for Vető.

As a next step, Commissioner Grnák called a meeting of the editorial commission of *Evangélikus Élet*. He demanded the publication of an article with a title suited for the Advent season, "Preparing the Way." The article contained sharp attacks against the leadership of the church. The editorial commission refused to print it, but the commissioner insisted. Ordass and Keken withdrew from the editorship. The name of Keken still appeared in the paper for months, however, which gave readers the impression that he had approved the unsigned article "Preparing the Way."

"Advent is the time when we prepare the way for the coming of the Lord," so the article began. "This means that we remove in our lives and in the life of the church everything that hinders us from receiving the Lord. . . . In this Advent season God has given us one more opportunity to put our business in order in the spirit of Advent." The article says of Ernő Mihályfi: "We note with pleasure and satisfaction that our church is once again led by its lawfully elected Church Inspector. . . . We have reason to hope that we shall see Lajos Vető as bishop at his side." When Grünvalszky resigned as the general secretary in 1956, the article said, he did so "under pressure from a convention that had been whirled up by the wind of the imminent counterrevolution." But now he, too, should begin his service again, "carried by the confidence of his church." All this happened, according to the article, "under the influence of the spirit of Advent. And we cannot stop halfway."

It was clear that stopping halfway was certainly not the intention of those in power. Commissioner Grnák established himself in the central office of the church. When Vető took over the diocese in the north, Grnák moved into the office of the southern district. Only Ordass and his diocese needed supervision.

Even though the negotiatons had failed, Horváth and Ordass met for further discussions. Horváth stressed that the government had to expect a "progressive" stance from church leaders in a Socialist system. He also mentioned that he had studied Ordass's remarks during his travels in the United States. (Ordass remembered two "journalists" who participated in his first press conference in New York and introduced themselves as representatives of the Hungarian embassy.) Ordass did not attack the Hungarian government in his remarks, but he also did not explicitly confirm that he was content about the situation of the church in Hungary. He mentioned neither the great results achieved by the construction of Socialism nor the optimism of the Hungarian people with regard to the future.

Horváth repeated that General Secretary Lund-Quist and Dr. Vajta had exercised an unfavorable influence on the church delegation. When Ordass asked for a reason for this accusation, Horváth referred to a corresponding remark by Professor Miklós Pálfy. He had to admit that the appointment of a commissioner meant curtailing the freedom of the church. But the church could have avoided the measure if it had not determined on its own the necessary changes in personnel! The state would respect the laws and rights of the church, but only insofar as they did not contradict the interests of the state. If church law contradicted the interests of the state, the churches would have to change their laws. Not even the appointment of a pastor in the smallest congregation was of no importance to the government, and the church leadership was obligated to steer the elections in such a way that the government's interests were not damaged. Reactionary pastors should not be preferred over "progressives." As soon as the ideal situation was established — that is, when all pastors were "progressive" — then the government would no longer meddle in matters of personnel. That was Horváth's conclusion.

Ordass could only reply that his church had always had to fight for its identity and integrity, whether it was during the bloody persecution of the Counter-Reformation or under the pressure of the Hapsburgs. Frequently it had to fight against "the spirit of the time." The Lutheran bishops had vowed in their oath of office to guard the integrity of the church. They could not remove themselves from this obligation at their own discretion.

After these discussions, Ordass gradually began to count on a new trial. But the authorities had learned a lesson from their blunder in 1948. This time they wanted to proceed without a trial.

Their first move was the announcement that the government would increase the salaries of the pastors in the northern district by 25 percent. Pastors in the southern district could also receive this increase — but only after Bishop Ordass "had straightened out his relationship with the government."

Nothing was gained by this attack. The voluntary gifts of the congregations more than compensated for what the pastors lost in the southern district. Moreover, a number of pastors in the northern district sent half of their additional pay from the government to their colleagues in Ordass's diocese. The bishop, who visited the pastors very often, heard only one complaint about the loss of the extra governmental pay.

The authorities soon made another attempt to get a reaction from the pastors in the southern district. The pastors of the territories of the eight seniors were asked to sign a resolution that was a vote of confidence in Ordass as bishop but that also asked him "to straighten out his relationship with the government." The resolutions, along with the signatures, were published in *Evangélikus Élet,* which increased the pressure on those who were obstinate.

Ordass tried to show cooperation by writing a letter asking the State Office of Church Affairs for "confirmation" that he exercised his office in harmony with the law. His letter was not answered. In order to avoid detrimental consequences for the pastors he made the request to undergo a disciplinary ecclesiastical investigation. This request also was not answered.

Ordass had emphasized several times that he would volunteer to resign if he felt certain that he no longer had the confidence of the pastors and congregations. The authorities now tried to use clergy conventions to obtain formal declarations of distrust against their bishop.

The first convention was staged in Budapest and chaired by the new senior Emil Koren. The main item on the agenda was a speech of Károly Grünvalszky, who sharply criticized Ordass's "adventurous politics" and questioned his ability as a bishop. He accused the representatives of the Lutheran World Federation of espionage and conspiracy and asserted that Ordass of course conspired with them. Obviously, Grünvalszky went too far, for no statement of distrust was issued.

A few days later, Ordass appeared uninvited at a similar convention called together by the senior in Pécs (Fünfkirchen), Zoltán Káldy, without informing his bishop. But the commissioner of the governmental church office, Grnák, and an official from the county had been invited there. Both sharply reproached Ordass. But here, too, no statement of distrust was issued. The participants even asked Ordass to conclude the convention with devotions.

A senior who dared to invite Ordass to be a speaker at one of these conventions was immediately deposed by the governmental church office.

Church leaders in the Scandinavian countries viewed with growing anxiety the pressure to which the Lutheran Church in Hungary was exposed. They addressed a joint letter to the director of the governmental church office, János Horváth, signed by the archbishops of Sweden and Finland, Yngve Brilioth and Ilmari Salomies, by Bishop Fuglsang Damgaard of Copenhagen, and by Johannes Smemo of Oslo. The letter said, among other things:

> It is our hope that the news about such heavy attacks against the spiritual freedom of the church is exaggerated, and we would be very grateful in this case to be informed about it. But if this is not the case we want to express our most serious misgivings. We are convinced, through our close connections that have grown for a long time with the mentioned church leaders, that they are not only persons with great spiritual integrity but also good and loyal citizens of their country. That is why we cannot be indifferent about the degree of our sister churches' ability to shape their spiritual and organizational affairs in freedom.

Although this letter to Horváth did not bring about an end to the attacks, Ordass was grateful to receive evidence once again of the significance of contacts beyond the national frontiers at a difficult time, and he felt strengthened through this solidarity with sister churches.

Only in June 1958 did the authorities stop attempting to rid themselves of Ordass with the help of the Lutheran Church. At that point they tried a different tactic. Horváth announced that the political authorities had not accepted the resignation of László Dezséry from the episcopal office in October 1956. Thus he was again reinstated in his office — that is, for two hours.

DEPOSED A SECOND TIME

Those two hours were used by Dezséry to deliver a speech that was printed in its entirety in *Evangélikus Élet*. At the end of his speech he declared that he retired from his office as bishop. *This* retirement, then, was accepted by the state authorities.

So Ordass was most conveniently deposed. The rulers had simply used the ordinance of March 1957 with retroactive authority as of October 1, 1956. It was the same ordinance that Horváth had earlier assured Ordass was not to apply to the Lutheran Church.

In his speech Dezséry attempted to influence church opinion and make acceptable the "new objective" of the Lutheran Church. Bishop Vető and Professor Pálfy published newspaper and magazine articles with the same intention. In these attacks Ordass was simultaneously called "high church" and "pietist." The intervention of the authorities was described as the "justified struggle of the state against the reactionaries" and as "very mild." The assistance of churches from abroad was connected with political ulterior motives, and the assembly at Galyatető was used by the foreigners for the preparation of the uprising of 1956. Ordass's radio speech of November 2 was asserted to be a political speech. Finally, Ordass was accused of forming a conspiratorial covenant with Cardinal Mindszenty.

There was no end to the accusations and charges with which Ordass and several other pastors, mentioned by name, were showered in these articles. They now had to count on punishment for their political — that is, "counter-revolutionary" — activity.

The authorities approved only a single candidate for the office of bishop, the senior of Pécs, Zoltán Káldy, who then assumed his office in the southern district on November 4, 1958.

Once again, the "Ordass affair" had come to an end.

27. An East European State Church

THE CHURCH workers who had been blacklisted during the negotiations in the fall of 1957 were all removed from office, one after the other. The original blacklist was supplemented with new names, among them those who had been mentioned in the speech of László Dezséry.

Three professors at the Theological Academy were quickly removed. Károly Karner and Dezső Wiczian were forced to retire. Jenő Sólyom, who had a large family, received employment in the central archives of the church. None of them was allowed to say farewell to students. They had to leave the Academy in a great hurry. Pastors who were blacklisted were often transferred to small, remote locations, far away from the capital. Some were given pastoral assignments with a great overload of work. Others again had to live and work with their large families under completely insufficient conditions.

György Kendeh was again forced to leave his office in Ordass's former congregation, Kelenföld. But this time he was saved from going to a labor camp. He had to take over the administration of a home for widows of pastors; but he was not allowed to preach there in the chapel. He was the only man among the staff of the home, and his duties included tending the vegetable garden and caring for the pigsty. The president of the Lutheran Association of Pastors, László Scholz, was forced to transfer to a congregation that could offer him and his family only a poor livelihood and conditions that nearly broke his health. Pál Zászkaliczky, who had previously been arrested in 1948, died shortly before his enforced transfer. Some of the best pastors of the church were removed in this manner from their active and lively congregations, and the congregations had to be content with pastors whom they would never have elected. The renewal movement in the church, which had been supported in the spring and summer even by the church leadership, among them also Bishop Vető, quickly melted away. In the following years, the church gave in more and more to the demands of the people's democratic government.

At the close of the 1940s the Communist Party had used the slogan "a free church in a free nation." The new constitution of Hungary contained a paragraph according to which church and state were separated. When the government abolished the obligatory teaching of religion in 1949, it did so by expressly appealing to this paragraph of the constitution. Now, ten years later, the rulers plotted a different course. Now they wanted to tie the church to the state as strongly as possible. In a speech at the beginning of 1958 János Horváth expressly said that the principle of "a free church in a free nation" was "reactionary."

The government secured for itself an effective control over the churches through the allotment of subsidies. In fact, according to the Agreement of 1948, the allotment of subsidies was supposed to have been reduced by 25 percent every fifth year in order to cease completely in 1968. But the Lutheran Church could renew the governmental subsidy every year through a formally submitted application. Professors of theology still received their full salaries from the government. In addition, every parish pastor received a subsidy in addition to his monthly salary. The church leadership decided who would receive the full amount of seven hundred forint and who had to be content with less.

In 1966, new laws were adopted by the legislative synod of the church. The laws were introduced with a "solemn declaration" of the synod members:

> With deep gratitude we want to be reminded that the Lord of history and of the church has given our church the possibility to begin a new life, after the liberation of our homeland from the inhumanity of fascism, from the injustice of the capitalist-feudalist system, and from religious oppression; and that he may spur on our church with his Holy Spirit to emulate our Lord Jesus Christ in service, in community with our people and all of humankind.

In the new church administration, power was concentrated at the top of the church structure, rather than resting with the congregations as it had for centuries. This enabled the government to have better control over the congregations and their pastors as well as the workers in the church and all its governing bodies. For example, the laws permitted the bishop to transfer pastors by force and to fill incumbencies "as church interests demand." What that meant was not clearly defined. Here the bishop could freely decide. But it is self-evident that "the good relationship with the state" would have to be protected. It was now church law that the church needed to have the permission of the authorities to fill leading positions.

From 1958 until his death in 1972, Ernő Mihályfi occupied the highest office in the church as general inspector of the whole church. He hardly participated in the life of the church, and he was rarely seen at public events. He also did not seek contact with guests from abroad. It was his personal desire to be buried "Communistically," without any church cooperation. Nevertheless, the Lutheran Church was represented in the guard of honor at his coffin, together with representatives of the general public. Bishop Káldy gave a speech in which he expressed gratitude to Mihályfi for having helped the church to find its place in a Socialist society.

Gradually the governmental church office was given very extensive powers of jurisdiction in order to control every church and the life of every congregation. The church office sent its representatives to all annual assemblies, whether of the whole church or of a single congregation. They were also present at other important sessions of the various ecclesiastical governing bodies, at clergy conventions, and at assemblies of seniors. The church office had a branch in every county capital. In addition, local police authorities maintained special offices for the supervision of the churches. Thus not only were the self-government and integrity of the church impugned but also its external freedom of movement was strongly curtailed.

When a congregational office needed a new seal, or a Catholic parish wanted to have new images of saints printed, the governmental church office had to give its permission. Circular letters of bishops needed the approval of the state and could be printed only with the permission of the church office. Pastors who were to teach religion had to receive a license, and candidates for ordination could only be ordained if they had first received approbation from the governmental church office.

As soon as Ordass was deposed, the commissioner who had been appointed by the state was recalled. But Ordass still remained "a thorn in the flesh" for the government even though he was removed from his office. The authorities claimed that no "Ordass problem" existed in the Lutheran Church. But the Hungarian partners in dialogue with guests from abroad themselves mentioned this "problem" in discussions, emphasizing to foreign guests that the bishop had to be deposed because of his obstinacy, his conservativism, and his inability to cooperate.

Pastors were strongly advised not to visit the deposed bishop. For some time, the street corner of Márvány Street in Budapest where Ordass lived was under surveillance. This sufficed to frighten many about what consequences visiting Ordass might bring for themselves, their families, and the educational possibilities for their children. The number who still dared to violate the prohibition of the church leadership steadily decreased.

Guests from abroad were informed that a visit with Ordass would be viewed as "an unfriendly gesture." The general secretary of the Lutheran World Federation, Kurt Schmidt-Clausen, had to forego a journey to Hungary in the spring of 1962 because he was unwilling to remove a visit with Ordass from his schedule. A guest from Denmark said that Ordass's successor became "furious" when he discovered that the Dane had visited Ordass. At his visit to Hungary in 1963 the president of the Lutheran World Federation, Fredrik A. Schiotz, had staged through a friend an "accidental" meeting with Ordass and his wife in the street. "Thus he could not decline" the invitation to a cup of coffee in Ordass's residence.

Despite the church leadership's efforts, Ordass was quite often visited by guests from abroad. But he always restricted himself to answering questions put by the visitor; he did not bring up sensitive issues himself. He did not apply for a telephone connection and did not open any mail from abroad. As the general assembly of the Lutheran World Federation in 1963 in Helsinki drew nearer, the bishops Vető and Káldy told the Federation that they regarded the invitation of Ordass, who was, of course, vice president, as "peculiar." When it became known that the Finnish archbishop, Martti Simojoki, had also sent a personal invitation to Ordass, the Finnish church was told the same thing. Already at the opening of the assembly Bishop Káldy announced at a press conference that the Hungarian delegation was in complete agreement with the authorities who refused to grant permission to leave the country to bishops Ordass and Túróczy. Túróczy spoke Finnish, his books had been translated into Finnish, and Helsinki University was to give him an honorary doctorate of theology during the assembly.

It is impossible for an outsider to decide whether or not the leaders of the church had been forced into this negative attitude toward Ordass only through the strong pressure of the government. They themselves always stressed, in all their utterances about Ordass and the situation in Hungary, that the church was free in both word and deed and that "with regard to the progressive stance" of the church there were no differences of opinion or a split in the church.

28. A Diary Loses Its Way

ONCE AGAIN removed from the center of current events, Ordass lived for twenty years in retreat in his flat on the fourth floor of the Márvány home for deaconnesses. After a few years, and only after interventions of church leaders from abroad, he received a suitable pension.

He now had the opportunity to dedicate himself to the study of Scandinavian literature and the work of translation. New manuscripts were constantly produced in the quiet flat. He did not know whether they would ever be printed or if they would remain in the drawer of his desk. Or would they perhaps end up in the archives or garbage cans of the security police, as did many of his manuscripts of the period before 1948?

He often visited his daughter and son-in-law in a village one hour north of Budapest. His son-in-law knew that he would never be granted a transfer to a larger congregation or to different employment. So he never applied for another pastoral position but instead remained as pastor in Nagybörzsöny. Ordass had his traditional place in the choir section of the church in Nagybörzsöny. His son-in-law once tried to use him as a substitute during a trip. To play it safe, he asked the bishop, Zoltán Káldy, for permisson. The answer was that this would only be allowed if Ordass himself would apply in writing for permission to preach.

Shortly before Christmas 1969, while visiting Nagybörzsöny, Ordass received a telegraphic demand to appear at the governmental church office. For ten years he had been treated as a "non-person" in the public life of the church. Now they wanted to speak with him.

He was received in the office by the deputy director of the Department for the Affairs of the Protestant Churches, István Straub, and his assistant. They began the conversation with general questions about Ordass's views about the church and church leadership. But soon the true reason for this questioning became apparent. A Finnish theology student had written a book about the Lutheran Church in Hungary. According to the views of the officials, the book disclosed a hostile attitude to the Hungarian government and the Lutheran Church leadership. The author cited Ordass as his source.

Ordass did not hide the fact that he knew well who the author, Antti Kukkonen, was. But he had not seen the book and could not pass judgment on it because he was not fluent in Finnish. Kukkonen had asked for information during a study trip in Hungary, and Ordass had given him the manuscript of his autobiography and some notes. He did not know how the theologian had used this material in his church-historical description. But he could vouch for the truth of his notes.

"How could you do something like this? To whom is it of any use?" Straub interrupted. This book had damaged the image of Hungary abroad, he continued. Moreover, many of Ordass's conversations with pastors had also damaged the image of the church.

Ordass looked almost pleased when he assured the two officials that only a few of his former pastors and co-workers still visited him. But his autobiography and notes contained only the truth; and if the author had incorrectly quoted them, or had misinterpreted them, he would be ready to amend misunderstandings. The officials did not want to doubt that, but thought that the truth was sometimes ambiguous and had to yield to peaceful coexistence as the higher interest of the state.

The one-and-a-half-hour conversation was polite and calm. But it showed that the authorities, in spite of everything, were not yet "finished" with the Lutheran Church. Ordass began to worry about the few friends who still visited him.

In the following weeks the governmental church office or one of the two bishops interrogated twenty-two pastors on the matter of "visits with Ordass." Remarkably often there was talk about a "conspiracy." It became evident that fifteen of the twenty-two pastors had never visited Ordass. Only a few had seen him during the past year. One interrogation even ended humorously. The person in question was asked how often he had visited Ordass in the past year. "Twice," he said. "And why?" Well, he wanted to bring his old friend something from the surplus of his garden, strawberries in the summer, apples in the fall. "And what did you talk about with him?" About nothing! For Ordass had been on a journey both times.

The two bishops claimed at the interrogations that foreign guests would be negatively influenced in their attitude toward Hungary by visits with Ordass. They cited as example the president of the Lutheran World Federation, Fredrik A. Schiotz, and General Secretary André Appel. The interrogated pastors could not know that Appel had never visited Ordass and that Schiotz had never brought up "delicate" questions in his conversations with him.

When the pastors were invited in the new year to the usual conventions by the seniors, "the Ordass problem" and the church's relation to him became the chief agenda item. As usual, the governmental church office was represented by one or more officials at these meetings. At the convention of Lutheran pastors in Budapest, both bishops were even present, together with Károly Grnák and István Straub from the church office.

Bishop Ernő Ottlyk was the spokesman who had replaced Lajos Vető as bishop of the northern diocese in 1967. Ottlyk drew up a list of twenty-one transgressions. Ottlyk's basic argument was that Ordass had surrendered his notes and his autobiography to foreigners illicitly. The church generously gave him a pension. Now he had abused that generosity by becoming active again. He had appeared as judge of the church and had criticized the church's leadership. He had greatly damaged the church. Until now the relationship between church and state had been positive and good. But the release of Ordass's autobiography had endangered this good relationship. The government had demonstrated great confidence in the pastors by allowing them to receive foreign literature and granting them trips abroad. But the state expected the pastors to prove themselves worthy of this confidence. Now they had to show their colors and openly present their point of view.

Ordass had created a scandal that was detrimental to the Hungarian church's relations with other churches. He had also attacked the Socialist fatherland, Ottyk continued. He had betrayed everything that is dear to the church. He had supported imperialism with his attitude and worked against Socialism. He had become a weapon in the hands of forces opposing Communism. He lived in Hungary, but he had committed treason.

Immediately after this introduction by Bishop Ottlyk there was a speech by Bishop Káldy. He began by stressing his wish that Ordass be informed about its content. Then he continued:

> It does not disturb us that Ordass's autobiography ended up abroad. This is but a symptom, a sign of the defamation and slander spread about us abroad. Ordass and his stooges also falsify history; they spread lies and hatred. That is why I now must retract what I once said about Ordass. Twelve years ago I told him face-to-face: I admire you, I like you, I esteem you highly. What I said then I must now retract.
>
> Why are we insulted and slandered by Ordass and his circle? Because we have put in order our relation to the government. We do not identify with atheism. But we cooperate with a state that openly professes atheism. This cooperation is not only possible; it is our task. Ordass, however, steers toward a self-determination of the church, toward confrontation, not toward cooperation but toward resistance. Here I must turn to my Marxist friends and thank them for their help in letting the church really be the church. They have helped us to do that.

After this powerful speech, the pastors were asked "to show their colors." One after the other had to stand up and state in the presence of the representatives of the church office that they could not identify themselves with Ordass and his conduct. Senior Várady read out a common resolution of the pastors in Budapest in which they unanimously distanced themselves from Ordass and expressed their confidence in the church leadership. Bishop Káldy found the text not detailed enough and proposed to condemn specifics of Ordass's behavior — namely, his release of his diary abroad. The bishops Káldy and Ottlyk and the seniors Koren and Várady were commissioned to draft the unanimously adopted resolution after the meeting.

Ordass could only pity his colleagues. They had distanced themselves from him under duress, in the presence of government officials who could make arbitrary decisions about their service and their whole existence. The whole procedure confirmed his conviction that the church was no longer free.

29. "Worthy of Your Calling"

In 1971 the University of Iceland celebrated its sixtieth anniversary. On this occasion it nominated several theologians and people in the church as honorary doctors of theology. Among them was Lajos Ordass. The commendation read:

> For his valuable engagement in international church labor, for his outstanding service in promoting interchurch and international relations, for his efforts to make known Christianity and the culture of the North of Europe, and not least for his translation of the significant work of Icelandic literature, the Passion Hymns.

Ordass was not allowed to travel to Reykjavik. But he was very pleased about this honor.

Several of his manuscripts had in the meantime been published, not in Hungary but in Western European countries. His meditations for every day of the year were published in Germany under the title *Food for Travel (Utravaló)*.

A guest from Norway had given him a Norwegian book of meditations for children, authored by Einar Lyngar. The guest had given the children's book to the bishop with some hesitation. But the bishop was immediately enthusiastic about it, quickly translated several meditations, and tested them on his grandchildren. His translation of the whole volume was published in Denmark, the first Christian book for children in Hungarian in decades. His translation of the three plays by Kaj Munk was also published there, with the help of (among others) the Danish ministry of culture.

Ordass was most pleased that his translation of Hallgrímur Pétursson's passion hymns from Iceland was published there; a second edition was even published within a few years. It was his greatest enterprise as a translator. In a learned introduction to the book he described the poet, his country, and thus also a Lutheran sister church that had been practically unknown before in areas where Hungarian was spoken.

He regularly read church papers and journals from the North and was very well informed about the situation of the church there. "Did you shave off your beard?" was the question with which he welcomed a guest from Norway whose face he had known before only from pictures in newspapers. He was busily occupied with signs of renewal in the life of Scandinavian sister churches; and he experienced a childlike pleasure when, for example, he received a letter from his former fellow student Bishop Bo Giertz, who reported about a successful student conference in Iceland in 1977 with more than 1,300 participants.

He was no less pleased when he heard about colleagues in the ministry in Hungary who used the limited opportunities of the church for work with children and youth. Whoever visited him received good advice and encouragement for further faithful service. He highly valued the new Bible translation that appeared in the 1970s in Hungary. But he also sharply criticized books that were printed in the name of the church but obviously served only the interests of the rulers.

Gradually he began again to open the mail he had received over the years from abroad, and he became a diligent correspondent. A Hungarian couple in London preserved hundreds of Ordass's densely written letters like a treasure. In one letter he congratulated a pastor on his ordination thirty years earlier; the pastor in question no longer even remembered the date. Grateful friends and colleagues acknowledged his faithfulness in telegrams and greetings that poured in from the whole world on his seventy-fifth birthday.

But his health was no longer good. After initial heart troubles in 1955, he suffered a severe heart attack at Easter 1962. He would hardly have survived it if his physician, the former mother-superior of the deaconess home Fébé, had not been nearby. He had another milder attack in 1973 but was able to recover quite quickly.

On a quiet day in August of 1978, after he had taken his walk and written several letters, his wife took the letters to the post office. When she returned she found him dead on the bed. He had become indisposed while she was absent, and he had just enough strength to lie down.

The couple would have celebrated their golden wedding anniversary in the following summer. A long journey together, during which they had encountered more storms than favorable weather, had suddenly ended.

His Icelandic Bible lay open on the table. It was his custom to read the Bible in the afternoon in a Scandinavian language. Now it was open to the Letter to the Ephesians, from which the text for his ordination fifty-four years earlier was taken: "I therefore, a prisoner for the Lord, beg you to lead a life worthy of the calling to which you have been called . . ." (4:1).

The time and place of the funeral were announced only orally. Nevertheless, about six hundred people found their way to Farkasrét Cemetery on August 19. A faithful friend from his former congregation in Cegléd rode nine hours on a motorcycle in order to learn the time and place of the funeral. The attending pastors had been instructed by the church leadership not to wear their vestments as was customary at the funeral of a pastor.

Despite all this, world Lutheranism was represented in great number. As soon as the death of the bishop became known abroad by telephone, the news traveled fast. Representatives of the staff and of the Executive Committee of the Lutheran World Federation came, as well as guests from the Lutheran churches in Austria, Germany, Norway, Sweden, Denmark, and England.

No speeches were given, according to Ordass's personal wish. A pastor from the congregation Ordass regularly attended, László Csengődy, presided. He prayed the following prayer at the coffin:

> We give you thanks, our Father in heaven, for victory over death through our Lord Jesus Christ; for his sacrificial death that gives us forgiveness of sins, life, and salvation. We also give you thanks for your messenger, death, which recalls us to the eternal kingdom of your grace and has taken from us our brother Dr. Lajos Ordass. Our hearts are heavy with pain and sorrow even though we know that we now surrender him into your hands in the conviction that he lived with you all his life as pastor and bishop in the bond of certainty of the final encounter with you. . . .
>
> At his coffin we give you thanks for the many signs of your love

that you have given him in rich measure — for your light with which he was allowed to shine in the merciless darkness of the war years. You were the source of his courage.

We give you thanks for the integrity in word and deed that you have granted him and that he has taught us.

In this time of mourning we also give you thanks for the pain that evokes the memories of tears and suffering in lonely prison cells and in lonely hearts. Through that, too, you want to teach and admonish us. But we give you thanks also for the gift of endless joy through prayer and the Word with which you have strengthened, heartened, and sustained our brother Lajos Ordass. . . .

May your goodness and justice crown his memory in what people say, in the service of his church, and in the stern hindsight of history. We give you thanks for his proclamation and for his silence, for the calm and deep wisdom that we felt mysteriously in his eyes, in his words, but also in his often frightening silence. All this is now enclosed by your love, by life not death. Lord, we know that, and we confess: [here follow the Beatitudes from Matthew 5].

A meager obituary appeared in the church paper *Evangélikus Élet* for "the pensioned Bishop Dr. Lajos Ordass." Listed were his most important personal data until 1948. The time thereafter was not touched on by a single word, except this sentence: "He held the office of bishop until his retirement."

30. Witness for Christ in Our Time

DESPITE THE meager obituary in *Evangélikus Élet,* Ordass was not forgotten beyond the borders of the country. Articles in his memory appeared everywhere, from the *Frankfurter Allgemeine Zeitung* to *Svenska Dagbladet* in Stockholm, and in congregational and church papers of many countries. In the Lutheran "Vinje Church" in Wilmar, Minnesota, his name is the last of a series of names beginning with Berggrav and Bonhoeffer commemorated as witnesses of Christ from two millennia written on a frieze that adorns the round nave. His portrait hangs in a parish hall in Buenos Aires. An artist in Cleveland, Ohio, created a series of reliefs with his features.

His stately figure drew attention to itself. Some Hungarians who encountered him found him too reserved and too taciturn. He did not make any gestures in the pulpit, and he did not interrupt those who spoke in assemblies. But one could say that he had a certain "charisma" and could fascinate people with his words and his appearance.

He never took the offensive. When he had thought over a matter, his opinion was as immovable as a rock. And he never left his opponents or his partners in negotiation in doubt about his opinion. That was his strength — but perhaps also his weakness.

He was not at all slow in discussion, and his facility in argument was such that even well-versed partners in dialogue and politicians occasionally were at a loss for an answer.

Especially later in his life, he was not able to make friends quickly, as did many others in Hungary. And some people were even afraid to get to know him, since any close link with him was risky. But he remained unswervingly loyal to his friends.

He was a man of the Bible. He missed nothing in his life more than the Bible that he was deprived of in the long months in prison.

He was also a man of prayer. He interceded not only for his family, his church, and his country but also for an unbelievably long list of friends and acquaintances in many countries whom he regularly remembered in his prayers. He was able to turn to his Savior with childlike simplicity and dialogue with him, as demonstrated in his book *At the Foot of the Cross*, which he had begun in solitary confinement.

His inner peace was attained through hard struggles and was purified by suffering. He was granted peace throughout his entire life, as he testified during his trial, immediately before his sentence. This peace was grounded in the cross of the Savior, which had been impressed on him already in childhood in the church of Torzsa. He fled to this cross during the years of difficult trials.

His inner peace did not remain unshakable. Although he received the strength to bear his own suffering, it was difficult for him to see others suffer for his sake. But even though he was alone, put out of the way, forced into silence, he could still do more for his church through his writings than others who had free access to the pulpits of the church.

When he stood in the pulpit for the last time, he cited at the end of his sermon the words of Jesus in Matthew 24:13: "But he who endures to the end will be saved." He became a witness of Christ for our time through his steadfastness.

His Savior had called him to serve. He could not betray his faith in him. He would rather go to prison than hand over the life and service of the church of Jesus Christ to a strange power.

He could not do otherwise.

Epilogue

NEARLY TWENTY years have passed since Lajos Ordass was buried at the Farkasrét Cemetery in Budapest. Much has changed since then in Hungary. But the relation of the Lutheran Church in Hungary to this important personality in its own history of this period is very unclear.

Six years after his death, the Lutheran World Federation held its Seventh Assembly in Budapest. On July 20, 1984, the day before the opening worship service, a small invited group convened at Ordass's grave. According to the English and German daily paper of the Assembly, Zoltán Káldy, at that time a member of the Executive Committee of the Federation, spoke of the "testament of Ordass" as well as of the "heritage of Ordass." The Hungarian edition of the same paper *(Napról Napra)* printed only an abbreviated version of this speech. And in the weekly edition of *Evangélikus Élet* there was no word at all about a testament or heritage of Ordass. Instead, the headline read: "Laying of a wreath at the grave of Lajos Ordass by *members of the Executive Committee*" (italics added), as if the event concerned only the Lutheran World Federation, but not the Lutheran Church in Hungary. *Evangélikus Élet* also did not mention that a wreath had been laid at the grave in the name of his church.

A few days later, the Assembly elected the holder of the bishop's office in the southern diocese of the Lutheran Church in Hungary, Zoltán Káldy, as president of the Lutheran World Federation.

In connection with the Assembly, a 120-page illustrated history of the Lutheran Church in Hungary, entitled *Hope Preserved* (Budapest, 1984; German edition, *Bewährte Hoffnung,* Erlangen, 1984), was published, written by the church historian Professor Tibor Fabiny. This book was distributed to all participants at the Assembly, as a gift from the host church. The events of 1956, when Bishops Vető and Dezséry withdrew from their offices and Bishop Ordass was able to resume his office after eight years, were mentioned in the book. In the book this is described with the sentence "Lajos Ordass resumed his earlier post *on his own initiative*" (p. 75, italics added) — "aus eigenem Entschluss" in the German version. The same expression was also used by the author in his presentation of his own book in *Lutheran World Information*.

In an open letter, the widow of Lajos Ordass protested against this insinuation. Her open letter was mentioned but not cited in *Lutheran World Information*. At a later time Professor Fabiny finally felt forced to publically correct his description of the events of 1956. Later it turned out that the expression "on his own initiative" was inserted into the manuscript — by Bishop Káldy.

In 1983 and 1986, the press office of the Lutheran Church published two editions of the memoirs of Pastor Gábor Sztehló, who had died in 1974. Sztehló had saved the lives of a great number of Jewish children during World War II. At five places in Sztehló's original notes Ordass is mentioned with words of praise for his assistance and the encouragement Sztehló received from him in his work. None of this is mentioned in the printed version.

Ordass's name had been taboo in the Hungarian church press during that whole period. In 1987 it seemed as if the silence had finally ended. "Since there are repeated inquiries about the person and service of the former Bishop Dr. Lajos Ordass at home and abroad," declared Bishop Gyula Nagy in the weekly paper *Evangélikus Élet* on April 5 of the same year, the church felt obligated to remember Ordass "with respect and reverence." There had been mistakes and blunders "on both sides unavoidably," "even some that have affected Bishop Ordass and his family, whose burden he took to the grave."

After this, Ordass's name was mentioned with reverence at some solemn occasions. Occasionally, memorial services were held at his grave. But those who hoped for an acknowledgment on the part of the church leadership that Lajos Ordass had been disgracefully treated by the church waited in vain.

In 1989, the year of the greatest revolutions of the postwar time in all of eastern Europe and, above all, also in Hungary, still no such admission was forthcoming. Irén Ordass, the widow of Bishop Ordass, wrote

EPILOGUE

several letters during this time to the church leadership, asking for a clear statement regarding the events of 1958, when her husband was deposed for the second time. Neither her letter of 1986 nor her open letter of 1987 received an appropriate response. The attempt of the Lajos Ordass Society, which was founded in 1989 in Budapest, to obtain a clear answer from the church leadership also failed. The church leadership even tried to pass off the responsibility onto the Communist authorities alone. They asked the Hungarian minister of justice to examine "the matter of the second, unjustified removal of Ordass" from the office of bishop in 1958, since "a rehabilitation on the part of the government regarding his removal and its consequences has not yet happened."

At the end of April 1990 the answer of the then still Communist minister of justice arrived. In his letter to Irén Ordass he stated that the removal of Bishop Ordass in 1958 had no legal foundation and that "his episcopal activity is to be regarded as uninterrupted since the year 1945." He begged her pardon (literally, "apologized") regarding these events in the name of the Hungarian government. The minister also addressed a similar letter to the administration of the Lutheran Church in Hungary.

Year after year passed, and no attempt was made by the Lutheran Church in Hungary to admit any guilt in "the case of Ordass." Finally, Irén Ordass found herself compelled to take one more initiative. In a letter of January 1995 she demanded that the disciplinary court of the Lutheran Church in Hungary make a decision concerning "rehabilitation" of her husband. She took this step even though she was of the opinion that the church leadership themselves should have taken such an initiative. The court decision was made on October 5, 1995. It stated that the resolution of the Lutheran Church in 1958 issuing a writ for election of a bishop was "illegal and therefore null and void," and that Lajos Ordass "was the legal bishop of the southern diocese [from his installation in 1945] until his death on August 14, 1978." This, of course, also entailed that Zoltán Káldy was an "illegal bishop" or what church historians call a usurper in the bishop's seat.

For eighteen years after the death of Bishop Ordass, his family, his friends, his church, and the general public at home and abroad had to wait for the time when he was not just shown an occasional mark of esteem, of "respect and reverence," but also received justice. Irén Ordass did not live to see her husband rehabilitated by his own church. She died four months before the decision of the church court was made, on June 3, 1995.

Sources and Literature

THE MATERIAL for this biography was collected over a period of several years. The most important sources were Ordass's own books, notes, and letters. First of all, there is his autobiography, completed in 1963, *A Small Mirror for Great Times (Nagy idők kis tükre)*, cited already in the preface of the present volume. An omnibus volume containing lectures, essays, and sermons of Ordass was published in Switzerland in 1982, with the title *Selected Writings (Válogatott írások)*. In addition there are fourteen other books by Ordass, including his translations of Scandinavian works, many of which contain extensive introductions.

A valuable source of information on events in Hungary's history consisted of Hungarian books, journals, and papers from 1945 on. In the comprehensive history books published in Hungary describing events in Hungary since World War II, Ordass is hardly mentioned, and the few mentions of him that do occur give only the government's views.

In addition, several archives in Western Europe were of value. The Söderblom archive in Uppsala is excellently arranged, and the material on Hungary can easily be traced. There is also valuable material in the archives of the Lutheran World Federation in Geneva. The late General Secretary Lund-Quist facilitated easy access to the material. Valuable material was also available in London, Strasbourg, and Munich.

Finally, I was also able to base my work on personal notes, memories, and correspondence. When my own bishop, Zoltán Túróczy, was in prison, I was ordained by Ordass in August 1946. I also had a series of conversations with Ordass in the 1970s during repeated visits to Hungary.

There is only scant literature in German or in any other Western European language that can provide information about Lajos Ordass.

Only three of Ordass's own books have been published in German or in English — namely, *At the Foot of the Cross* (meditations for Lent, Minneapolis, 1958), *The Indictment* (a short novel, Minneapolis, 1968), and *I Cannot Pray* (*Ich kann nicht beten*, Gladbeck, 1968). All three books appeared anonymously.

The two books of the Reformed church historian Mihály Bucsay, entitled *History of Protestantism in Hungary* (*Geschichte des Protestantismus in Ungarn*, Stuttgart, 1959) and *Protestantism in Hungary 1521-1978* (*Der Protestantismus in Ungarn 1521-1978*, Vienna, Cologne, Graz, 1977-79), deal mainly with the Reformed Church in Hungary and the time before 1945; they do not even mention the name Lajos Ordass. The latter book was published with much financial assistance from a series of governmental, scientific, and ecclesiastical groups.

Ernő Ottlyk, formerly professor of church history at the Lutheran Theological Academy in Budapest, later bishop (1967-1980) of the northern district of the Lutheran Church in Hungary, wrote a book, published in East Germany, entitled *The Way of a Protestant Church in Socialism* (*Der Weg einer evangelischen Kirche im Sozialismus*, Berlin, 1982). As is written on the back cover, this book describes "the struggle between what is old and new in the church and illustrates that the borderline is not between believers and unbelievers, but between the enemies and friends of Socialism." The festival publication of his successor in the chair of church history, Tibor Fabiny, *Hope Preserved* (Budapest 1984; *Bewährte Hoffnung*, Erlangen, 1984), is also written in the spirit of the "official" historiography of this period.

The comprehensive study of Vilmos Vajta, *The "Diaconical Theology" in the Social System of Hungary* (*Die "diakonische Theologie" im Gesellschaftssystem Ungarns*, Frankfurt, 1987), not only offers a solidly documented analysis of a theological system closely linked with the name of Zoltán Káldy but also contains an extensive report about "the case of Ordass" (pp. 19-35).

Among the publications of the Roman Catholic Center of Documentation (IDOC) in Rome, the pamphlet *Churches in Socialism* contains several important documents concerning the Protestant churches in Hungary.

The letter of Lajos Ordass to the president of the State Office of Church Affairs, János Horváth, dated October 25, 1957, is reprinted in full in Gerd Hamburger's book *Faith Behind Bars* (*Glaube hinter Gittern*, Vienna, Munich, 1979, pp. 74-89). The same author also included a short biography of Ordass in his collection *Persecuted Christians* (*Verfolgte Christen*, Graz, Vienna, Cologne, 1977, pp. 80-86).

Attention should also be drawn to the continual reports of various information services and yearbooks: for example, *Hungarian Church Press Service*, formerly *Hungarian Church News Service* (not because of its reliability but because of its documentary character); *East Church Information* (*Ostkirchliche Information*, Hannover); *Church in the East* (*Kirche im Osten*, Münster, Westphalia); and *Faith in the Second World* (*Glaube in der 2. Welt*, Zollikon).

Concerning the Roman Catholic Church in Hungary, the *UKI Press Service (UKI Pressedienst)* of the Hungarian Church-Sociological Institute in Vienna is of special significance, as are several of its publications, especially Emmerich András and Julius Morel, *Taking Stock of Hungarian Catholicism* (*Bilanz des ungarischen Katholizismus*, Munich, 1969), and the collection of essays in *Church in Transition* (Vienna, 1983).

Chronology

1901 Lajos Wolf (later Ordass) is born on February 6, in Torzsa, southern Hungary (now Yugoslavia).
1912 Lajos moves to Verbász in September to attend the gymnasium.
1916 Lajos's mother dies on May 25.
1918 The territory to which Torzsa belongs (Bácska) is annexed by Yugoslavia; Lajos remains in Hungary.
1920 Lajos begins to study theology in Budapest in September.
1922 Lajos spends two semesters at the Theological Faculty in Halle.
1924 Lajos is ordained by Bishop Sándor Raffay as curate (vicar) on October 5.
1927 Lajos spends two semesters studying in Sweden.
1929 Lajos applies for and is given an assignment as military chaplain on June 1. His marriage with Irén Kirner takes place on August 20.
1930 The World Assembly for Diaconia takes place in Uppsala in August. On September 1 Lajos is given the assignment of "mission developer" in the church district of Bánya.
1931 Lajos is installed as pastor of the congregation in Cegléd on June 14.
1937 Lajos is elected senior of the "middle Pest" district on August 5.
1941 Lajos is installed as pastor of the congregation of Kelenföld in Budapest on November 2.
1944 The occupation of Hungary by German troops begins on March 19. Lajos Wolf changes his name to Lajos Ordass.

1945 Ordass is installed as bishop in the church district of Bánya on September 27.
1947 Ordass conducts a lecture tour in Scandinavia, Switzerland, and the United States from February 23 to July 27. In July he is elected vice president of the Executive Committee in the Lutheran World Federation.
1948 Ordass is arrested on August 24 and released one day later. On August 30 he is given the deadline of September 8 to resign. On September 8 he is arrested and indicted for "currency fraud." On October 1 he is sentenced to two years in prison. On December 14 the Agreement between the Hungarian People's Republic and the Lutheran Church in Hungary is signed.
1950 Bishop Túróczy visits Ordass in prison on January 8. Ordass enters solitary confinement in Vác on March 15. The special court of the Lutheran Church deposes Ordass on April 1. Ordass is released from prison on May 30. László Dezséry takes over the bishop's office in October.
1951 The governmental State Office of Church Affairs is established.
1952 The four dioceses of the Lutheran Church in Hungary are merged into two: North and South. The bishops are Lajos Vető and László Dezséry.
1956 The prospect of Ordass's rehabilitation is held out on July 11. On August 4 an agreement is reached between the Hungarian authorities and the representatives of the Lutheran World Federation about his rehabilitation. On October 5 the Supreme Court of the Hungarian People's Republic annuls the verdict of October 1, 1948. On October 8 the Disciplinary Court of the Lutheran Church annuls the verdict of April 1, 1950. Ordass preaches publicly for the first time in eight years on October 14. An uprising in Hungary takes place on October 23. Dezséry resigns on October 30, and Ordass resumes his office. Soviet intervention in Hungary begins November 4.
1957 Ordass speaks at the Third Assembly of the Lutheran World Federation in Minneapolis on August 15; he is reelected as vice president of the Executive Committee. Ordass writes to the governmental church office October 25; negotiations begin. The authorities interrupt the negotiations on November 26.
1958 Ordass is deposed for the second time on June 18; the "legal basis" is the ordinance of the Presidential Council of the Hungar-

ian People's Republic (43/1957). Zoltán Káldy is "elected" to be Ordass's successor on November 4.
1962 Ordass suffers a severe heart attack at Easter.
1963 The Fourth Assembly of the Lutheran World Federation is held in Helsinki. Ordass is not granted permission to attend.
1966 New church laws are adopted by the Lutheran Church in Hungary.
1969 Ordass is interrogated in the governmental church office on December 4.
1971 Ordass is granted an honorary doctor of theology degree by the University of Iceland.
1973 Ordass suffers a mild heart attack.
1978 Ordass dies of heart failure on August 14. The funeral is held at Farkasrét Cemetery in Budapest on August 19.

Index of Names

Aasgaard, Johan A. (1876-1965; President of the Norwegian Lutheran Church in the USA), 52
Ammundsen, Valdemar (1875-1936; professor of church history, bishop [Denmark]), 25
Appel, André (b. 1921; Church president [France], General Secretary of the Lutheran World Federation), 149
Aulén, Gustaf (1879-1977; professor of systematic theology, Bishop of Strängnäs [Sweden]), 24, 38, 88

Barstad, Johannes (1857-1931; provost, composer of hymns [Norway]), 113
Bártfay-Kelló, Gusztáv (Lutheran pastor), 105
Bereczky, Albert (1893-1955; Reformed bishop), 63, 73, 83
Berggrav, Eivind (1884-1959; Bishop of Oslo [Norway]), 52, 53, 55, 110, 155
Bethlen, Gábor (1580-1629; Duke of Transylvania), 24
Björkquist, Manfred (1884-1985; Bishop of Stockholm [Sweden]), 25
Böhm, János (brother-in-law of Lajos Ordass), 45
Bonhoeffer, Dietrich (1906-1945), 155
Borbándi, Gyula (b. 1919; historian), 68
Brilioth, Yngve (1891-1959; Archbishop of Uppsala [Sweden]), 140

Cederberg, Daniel (1908-1969; pastor [Sweden]), 111, 112
Csengődy, László (1925-1991; pastor in Budahegyvidék), 153

Darvas, József (1912-1973; writer, church inspector), 68, 74, 76, 93, 103, 108, 116, 122, 124, 136
Deák, János (1883-1961; professor of Old Testament), 16, 19, 20, 99
Dedinszky, Gyula (1905-1995; pastor in Békéscsaba), 24, 27, 30
Dezséry, László (1914-1977; campus pastor, bishop), 44, 79, 93, 94, 108, 109, 110, 111, 112, 113, 117,

INDEX OF NAMES

121, 123, 124, 131, 140, 141, 142, 158
Dinnyés, Lajos (1901-1961; prime minister), 76
Dobschütz, Ernst von (professor of church history), 18

Ehrenström, Nils (1903-1984; secretary of studies [Geneva], professor of theology [Sweden; USA]), 58
Eissfeldt, Otto (1887-1973; professor of Old Testament), 17
Empie, Paul (1909-1979; General Secretary of the Lutheran Council in the USA), 127

Fabiny, Tibor (b. 1924; professor of church history), 157, 158
Famler, Gustav Adolf (Lutheran pastor in Torzsa), 6
Feine, Paul (1859-1933; professor of New Testament), 17
Ficker, Johannes (1861-1944; professor of church history), 18
Franz Joseph II (1830-1916; emperor [from 1848] of the Hapsburg Empire), 1
Fry, Franklin C. (1900-1968; President of the United Lutheran Church in America and of the Lutheran World Federation), 52, 116, 129
Fuglsang-Damgaard, Hans (1890-1979; Bishop of Copenhagen [Denmark]), 126, 140

Gaudy, László (1895-1976; pastor, teacher of religion), 68
Geduly, Henrik (1866-1937; Lutheran bishop), 21

Gerő, Ernő (1898-1976; General Secretary of the Communist Party in Hungary), 121
Giertz, Bo (b. 1905; Bishop of Gothenburg [Sweden]), 26, 41, 129, 138, 152
Grnák, Károly (State Commissioner of the Lutheran Church in Hungary, 1957-58), 137-38, 140, 149
Groó, Gyula (1913-1989; General Secretary of the Lutheran Church in Hungary, professor of theology), 102
Grösz, József (1887-1961; Archbishop of Kalocsa), 103, 115
Grüber, Heinrich (1891-1975; provost in Berlin), 128
Grundtvig, N. F. S. (1783-1872; poet and theologian, founder of the folk schools for higher education [Denmark]), 25
Grünvalszky, Károly (1913-1996; pastor, General Secretary of the Lutheran Church in Hungary), 48, 121, 135, 137, 139
Gunkel, Hermann (1862-1932; professor of Old Testament), 17
Gustavus Adolfus II (1594-1632; king of Sweden), 24
Gyimesi, Károly (pastor in Budapest), 79, 93
Gyöngyösi, Vilmos (pastor in Budapest and Frankfurt), 79, 93

Hitler, Adolf, 36
Holmquist, Hjalmar (1873-1945; professor of church history [Sweden]), 24
Horthy, Miklós (1868-1957; head of state, 1930-44 [Hungary]), 36
Horváth, János (director of the state office of church affairs), 116,

117, 121, 123, 124, 131, 132, 135, 136, 137, 138, 140, 141, 143
Hultgren, Gunnar (1902-1991; Archbishop of Uppsala [Sweden]), 26
Hylander, Ivar (1900-1982; Bishop of Luleå [Sweden]), 26

Jeremiasson (shoemaker in Lund [Sweden]), 26
Johansson, Harry (1905-1983; director of Swedish Church Aid), 26
Johnson, Gisle (1876-1946; Norwegian mission pastor in Budapest), 39
Joseph II (1741-1790; emperor [from 1765] of the Hapsburg Empire), 1, 7

Kádár, János (General Secretary of the Hungarian Communist Party), 107, 130
Káldy, Zoltán (1919-1987; Lutheran bishop), 140, 141, 144, 145, 147, 150, 157, 158, 159
Kapi, Béla (1879-1957; Lutheran bishop), 70, 71, 73, 74, 93
Kardos, János (Ordass's defense attorney), 82, 83
Karlström, Nils (1902-1987; cathedral provost [Sweden]), 26
Karner, Károly (1897-1984; professor of New Testament), 19, 37, 142
Keken, András (1909-1974; pastor of the main church at Deáktér, Budapest), 91, 92, 105, 108, 109, 116, 119, 137
Kemény, Lajos (1883-1953; provost in Budapest), 44, 62, 108
Kendeh, György (b. 1912; pastor at Kelenföld, Budapest), 33, 92, 105, 108, 109, 116, 119, 137, 142

Kirner, Gusztáv (Lutheran pastor), 20, 21, 23, 29
Kirner, Irén. *See* Ordass, Irén
Koren, Emil (pastor in Budapest, vicar of the bishop), 139, 150
Kossa, István (1904-1965; Communist politician, minister of church affairs), 82, 114
Kossuth, Lajos (1802-1894; Hungarian hero of freedom), 69
Kovács, Béla (1908-1959; member of parliament), 64
Kovács, Sándor (1869-1942; professor of church history, bishop), 19, 35, 99
Khruschchev, Nikita, 115
Kukkonen, Antti (student of theology [Finland]), 148

Langlet, Valdemar (1872-1960; representative of the Swedish Red Cross in Budapest), 38, 39
Leskó, Béla (1922-1988; president of the theological faculty in Buenos Aires), 56, 77
Lilje, Hanns (1899-1977; bishop, President of the Lutheran World Federation), 111, 116
Lindström, Martin (b. 1904; Bishop of Lund [Sweden]), 26
Loofs, Friedrich (1858-1923; professor of theology), 17
Lunde, Johan (1866-1938; Bishop of Oslo [Norway]), 30
Lund-Quist, Carl E. (1908-1965; General Secretary of the Lutheran World Federation [USA]), 117, 124, 128, 136, 138
Luther, Martin, 18, 20
Lutz, Carl (1895-1975; Swiss diplomat in Budapest), 38

INDEX OF NAMES

Lyngar, Einar (1907-1990; pastor [Norway]), 151

Margócsy, Emil (prosecutor in the disciplinary procedure against Ordass), 102, 106
Maria Theresa (1717-1780; empress [from 1740] of the Hapsburg Empire), 20
Masaryk, Jan (1886-1948; secretary of state of Czechoslovakia), 67
Mekis, Ádám (pastor), 135
Melanchthon, Philipp, 17
Michelfelder, Sylvester C. (1889-1951; General Secretary of the Lutheran World Federation [USA]), 54, 67, 77, 103, 128
Mihályfi, Ernő (1898-1972; writer, general inspector), 67, 68, 69, 70, 72, 73, 76, 78, 79, 93, 108, 120, 122, 123, 132, 136, 137, 144
Miklós, Imre (director of the state office of church affairs), 116, 117
Mindszenty, József (1892-1975; Archbishop of Esztergom, cardinal), 89, 94, 103, 115, 122, 141
Munk, Kaj (1898-1944; pastor, poet [Denmark]), 41, 126, 151
Münnich, Ferenc (1886-1967; Communist politician), 131
Murányi, György (Lutheran pastor), 105

Nagy, Ferenc (1904-1979; prime minister of Hungary), 64
Nagy, Gyula (Lutheran bishop), 158
Németh, Károly (Lutheran pastor), 74
Nestle, Eberhard (1851-1913; professor of New Testament), 18
Nygren, Anders (1900-1978; professor of systematic theology, Bishop of Lund [Sweden]), 24, 53, 111

Ordass, Barnabás (1930-1995; son of Lajos Ordass), 29, 109, 110
Ordass, Erzsébet (1942-1996; daughter of Lajos Ordass), 29
Ordass, Irén (1905-1995; wife of Lajos Ordass), 20, 29, 40, 41, 42, 44, 67, 88, 95, 158, 159
Ordass, Sára (b. 1933; daughter of Lajos Ordass), 29
Ordass, Zsuszanna (b. 1937; daughter of Lajos Ordass), 29, 33
Ortutay, Gyula (1910-?; writer, minister for church and education), 64, 75, 91
Ottlyk, Ernő (1917-1995; Lutheran bishop), 149, 150

Pálfy, Miklos (professor of Old Testament), 110, 135, 138, 141
Péter, General Gábor (head of security police), 107
Pétursson, Hallgrímur (1614-1674; pastor, poet [Iceland]), 112, 152
Pósfay, György (b. 1921; pastor, Secretary for Latin America in the Lutheran World Federation), 56, 77
Prőhle, Károly (b. 1911; professor of New Testament), 105

Radvánszky, Albert (1880-1963; general inspector of the Lutheran Church in Hungary), 70, 71, 77, 80, 81, 92, 93
Raffay, Sándor (bishop), 16, 22, 23, 25, 26, 28, 37, 39, 43, 44, 61, 99
Rajk, László (1909-1949; minister of the interior), 103, 115
Rákosi, Mátyás (1892-1971; General

Secretary of the Hungarian Communist Party), 67, 70, 71, 75, 94, 95, 102, 105, 107, 108, 121
Ravasz, László (1882-1975; Reformed bishop), 39
Reök, Iván (surgeon, general inspector of the Lutheran Church), 68, 70, 71, 73, 93, 96, 102, 103, 104, 105, 106, 108
Rodhe, Edvard (Bishop of Lund [Sweden]), 26
Rőzse, István (Lutheran pastor), 104

Salomies, Ilmari (1893-1973; archbishop [Finland]), 140
Schartau, Henrik (1757-1825; pastor [Sweden]), 25
Schiotz, Fredrik A. (1901-1989; President of the American Lutheran Church and of the Lutheran World Federation), 145, 149
Schmidt-Clausen, Kurt (1920-1993; General Secretary of the Lutheran World Federation), 145
Scholz, László (b. 1911; pastor, hymn writer, President of the Hungarian Lutheran Pastors' Association), 142
Schweitzer, Albert (1875-1965), 25
Serédi, Jusztinián (1884-1945; Archbishop of Esztergom, cardinal), 39
Sigurdsson, Sigurdgeir (bishop [Iceland]), 112
Simojoki, Martti (1908-?; archbishop [Finland]), 145
Smemo, Johannes (1898-1973; Bishop of Oslo [Norway]), 140
Söderblom, Nathan (1866-1931; Archbishop of Uppsala [Sweden]), 25, 26, 99

Sólyom, Jenő (1904-1976; professor of church history), 142
Stalin, Josef, 107, 115, 122
Steinmetz, Paula. *See* Wolf, Paula
Stephan, Horst (1873-1954; church historian), 18
Straub, István (employee of the state office of church affairs), 148, 149
Szabó, József (1902-1982; Lutheran bishop), 69, 74, 75, 96, 108, 135
Szálasi, Ferenc (1897-1946; National-Socialist "leader of the nation"), 71
Sztehló, Gábor (pastor), 158

Tessényi, János (Methodist pastor), 66, 67
Tildy, Zoltán (1889-1961; Reformed pastor, president of the Hungarian Republic, 1946-48), 46, 69, 76
Tito, Josip (1892-1980; Communist dictator in Yugoslavia), 115
Túróczy, Zoltán (1893-1971; bishop), 61, 68, 73, 74, 75, 78, 79, 94, 95, 96, 102, 104, 105, 108, 123, 124, 137, 145

Vajta, Vilmos (b. 1918; professor of theology), 56, 76, 77, 126, 136, 138
Várady, Lajos (Lutheran provost in Budapest), 150
Vargha, Sándor (1905-1990; General Secretary of the Lutheran Church in Hungary), 80, 81, 92, 93
Vető, Lajos (1904-1989; bishop), 104, 108, 110, 111, 117, 120, 122, 123, 124, 135, 136, 137, 138, 141, 143, 145, 149, 158

INDEX OF NAMES

Visser 't Hooft, W. A. (1900-1986; General Secretary of the World Council of Churches), 116
Vladár, Gábor (church inspector), 70

Wallenberg, Raoul (1912-?; Swedish diplomat), 38
Wentz, Abdel Ross (1883-1976; Vice President of the Lutheran World Federation), 52, 54
Wick, Ruth (officer of the Lutheran Council in the USA), 128
Wiczián, Dezső (1901-1961; professor of church history), 142
Wolf, Arthur, Sr. (d. 1935; father of Lajos Ordass), 1, 3, 4, 8, 10, 11-12
Wolf, Arthur, Jr. (brother of Lajos Ordass), 3

Wolf, Ilona (sister of Lajos Ordass), 3, 19
Wolf, János (brother of Lajos Ordass), 3, 21
Wolf, Matild (sister of Lajos Ordass), 3
Wolf, Paula (d. 1916; mother of Lajos Ordass), 2, 3, 12
Wolf, Paula (sister of Lajos Ordass), 3, 11, 19

Zászkaliczky, Pál (1905-1962; provost, vicar of the bishop), 105, 142
Zeuthen, Mogens (1918-1973; pastor, Secretary for Minority Churches in the Lutheran World Federation [Denmark]), 124